OSPREY AIRCRAFT OF THE ACES • 33

Nieuport Aces of World War 1

SERIES EDITOR: TONY HOLMES

OSPREY AIRCRAFT OF THE ACES • 33

Nieuport Aces of World War 1

Norman Franks

OSPREY
AVIATION

Front cover
Charles Nungesser not only recorded 43 official combat victories
between 1915-18, but managed to
break every major bone in his body
at least once due to crashes and
combats. His first fighter *escadrille*
was N65 in 1916, and he continued
to fly Nieuport Scouts in 1917 when
attached to V116. While almost all
his aircraft carried the famous black
heart, with skull and crossbones,
coffin and candlesticks, on the fuselage sides, he also had broad red,
white and blue bands across the
upper surfaces of all wings and on
the fuselage top decking. A number
of French Nieuports carried these
because the wing configuration of
the aircraft was often confused with
the Albatros Scout. It is said that
Nungesser had reacted to an attack
by a British machine and shot it
down, after which he made sure
nobody would make the same mis-
take again. This particular Nieuport
25 (N1895 – a number he used on
other Nieuports) is seen in action
with a German two-seater in May
1917, a month in which he claimed
six German machines (*cover artwork by Iain Wyllie*)

Back cover
Marius 'Marc' Ambrogi flew
Nieuport Scouts with N90, scoring
several early victories with the type
before downing a further 11 kills on
SPADs. He had to wait until 1940 to
score his 15th victory, when he
destroyed a Dornier Do 17 whilst
flying a Bloch 152 during the Battle
of France

First published in Great Britain in 2000 by Osprey Publishing
Elms Court, Chapel Way, Botley, Oxford, OX2 9LP
E-mail: info@ospreypublishing.com

© 2000 Osprey Publishing

ISBN 1 85532 961 1

Edited by Tony Holmes
Page design by TT Designs, T & B Truscott
Cover Artwork by Iain Wyllie
Aircraft Profiles by Harry Dempsey
Scale Drawings by Mark Styling
Origination by Grasmere Digital Imaging, Leeds, UK
Printed through Bookbuilders, Hong Kong

00 01 02 03 04 10 9 8 7 6 5 4 3 2 1

ACKNOWLEDGEMENTS
The author wishes to thank Greg VanWyngarden, Mike O'Connor,
Jon Guttman, Stuart Leslie, Greg Alegi and Walter Pieters for their help
with the compilation of this work.

EDITOR'S NOTE
To make this best-selling series as authoritative as possible, the editor would
be extremely interested in hearing from any individual who may have relevant
photographs, documentation or first-hand experiences relating to the elite
pilots, and their aircraft, of the various theatres of war. Any material used
will be fully credited to its original source. Please write to Tony Holmes at
10 Prospect Road, Sevenoaks, Kent, TN13 3UA, Great Britain, or by e-mail
at tony.holmes@osprey-jets.freeserve.co.uk

For a catalogue of all titles published by Osprey Military, Aviation and Automotive please write to:
Osprey Direct UK, P.O. Box 140, Wellingborough, Northants NN8 4ZA, UK
E-mail: **info@ospreydirect.co.uk**
Osprey Direct USA, P.O. Box 130, Sterling Heights, MI 48311-0130, USA
E-mail: **info@ospreydirectusa.com**
Or visit us at **www.ospreypublishing.com**

CONTENTS

SETTING THE SCENE

The late afternoon sky of 2 July 1916 had taken on a hazy look after the cloudiness of the morning. The Royal Flying Corps (RFC) had patrols out looking for hostile aircraft. No 11 Sqn had one of its Nieuport Scout at 10,000 ft escorting four Royal Aircraft Factory FE 2b two-seat pushers near Mercatel, having crossed the trenches which stretched from the North Sea coast to Switzerland. It was 1730 British time, and the keen eyes of the Nieuport pilot had already spotted four Roland C II two-seat fighters heading towards the FEs. As they closed, two of the FEs broke formation to engage, and so did the Nieuport.

Machine guns rattled and engines strained as pilots hauled their aircraft round in the new third dimension of air warfare. One of the Rolands staggered away to crash, hit by the front gunner of one of the FEs. Meanwhile, the Nieuport pilot dived and fired a drum of Lewis gun ammunition into the near side of another of the C IIs. It also dived, and the British pilot watched until the Rolaand crashed on the Mercatel to Arras road.

Less than half an hour later, the FEs having headed back across the lines, the Nieuport pilot, continuing to patrol alone, saw a German two-seater Aviatik over Lens. He edged towards it, hoping to gain a favourable position from which to attack without either of the two German airmen seeing him. The British pilot was closing slightly below and behind, trying to keep in the blind-spot under the two-seater's tail. Getting to within 20 yards, the pilot pulled the firing lever but his gun cable jammed.

Still remaining behind the unsuspecting Aviatik, the British pilot took the alternate course of action of dropping below the target, pulling down the Lewis gun, situated on the top wing in order to fire over the whirling blades of the propeller, and grabbing the handle-grip, his gloved finger squeezed the trigger. Three-quarters of the drum's 0.303-in bullets rattled up into the belly of the Aviatik, the aiming point being the crew compartments. There was no armour to protect the two men, only wood and fabric.

Albert Ball flew Nieuports with Nos 11 and 60 Sqns during 1915-16. Often flying alone, he had achieved 31 victories by the end of September 1916. On returning to France in 1917, as a flight commander with No 56 Sqn, Ball flew SE 5s but also had his own Nieuport Scout (B1522) in which he claimed his 32nd victory. With a score of 44 claims, he was killed on 6 May 1917 and was later awarded a posthumous Victoria Cross

The Aviatik staggered, began to side-slip away and down, then tumbled earthwards from 11,000 ft, finally smashing into the ground below, completely wrecked. Because of a lack of German casualties this day, it has to be assumed that the German airmen, possibly injured, did at least survive their encounter with one of the up and coming British ace pilots of the RFC, Lt Albert Ball. This late afternoon's work had brought his score of victories to seven, six having now been achieved flying the Nieuport.

WAR IN THE AIR

Before getting into this new series on World War 1 aces, perhaps the readers should be reminded, or for those new to World War 1 air fighting, just how these airmen saw and found their new environment. As many of today's enthusiasts were brought up on the aerial warfare of World War 2, it is all too easy to be confused by mixing these later air battles with those of World War 1. Another easy stumbling block is the benefit of hindsight.

The latter hinders the ability of understanding what went on at a certain period, because one knows how things turned out, or developed, weeks or months later. The true historian has to try very hard to understand things while ignoring what came later. As an example, if one reads about Manfred von Richthofen's early fighting career, it is easy to fall into the trap of knowing how good he probably was, knowing that he was to achieve 80 victories before he too fell in combat. But when he was a minor ace with six or seven victories, he was no better than three or four other *Jasta* 2 pilots at that time.

The term 'victories' is emotive too. Again one can easily fall into the trap of seeing World War 1 victories in the same light as World War 2. However, they were very different. In World War 1 everything was a learning curve. When that war began, air combat victories had not been invented. It was only when pilots began to shoot or force down an opposing aeroplane that someone 'invented' air victories. This in turn, like so many things, was pounced upon by the 'media', and soon the prowess of a fighting pilot was measured by the number of opponents he brought down. This became true whatever his nationality – French, British or German. They became the 'knights of the air'. It is open to debate whether this was good for each countrys' air service, or if helped to paint a false picture in relation to other airmen in bombers or reconnaissance squadrons, but history has preserved this yardstick, and we have to live with it.

So, victories in the beginning were mainly just that – being victorious over an opponent, but not necessarily 'destroying' him. In World War 2 victories meant aircraft destroyed, but in World War 1 it meant those aircraft destroyed, damaged and/or forced to land, or those thought to have been destroyed. They also included kite balloons – those observation 'gasbags' that, tethered to the ground, went aloft with one or more observers in a basket to view the enemy's positions for troop movements, or gun batteries.

Some of these 'victory' types will be mentioned in the text of this series, but the aforementioned usually refers to the British Royal Flying Corps, Royal Naval Air Service (RNAS) and later the Royal Air Force (RAF). The French and Germans only counted aircraft destroyed in their aces' scores, whereas a British ace with, say, ten victories may have his tally made up of six destroyed, one balloon and three 'out of control' – the 'probables' of World War 2.

A FIGHTER'S FIGHTER

When World War 1 began, each side had a variety of aeroplanes. Neither side started off with squadron of dedicated machines – they flew what they had, and what they were later given. Once the airmen of both sides began to encounter each other over the trench system which ended open warfare, and started four years of near stalemate, each side's young men being launched against barbed wire and machine-guns, often in a quagmire of mud of a shattered countryside, they searched for a method of damaging each other. Both sides knew the value of reconnaissance, once the traditional cavalry could no longer operate, and each side needed to stop the opposition from either seeing what was happening on their side of the lines, or if too late, to stop them getting the information back. Thus air fighting began.

Each side rapidly tried to develop a suitable method of placing a machine gun in an aeroplane, but the propeller, stuck right in front of the pilot, was the problem. To get over this, guns were mounted to fire obliquely, or metal plates fixed to the propeller blades, in order to deflect bullets fired through them. Another development was to place the propeller at the back, so the forward firing area was clear – the 'pusher' concept.

Yet another way was to fix the machine gun on the top wing, angled to fire forward and slightly downwards. In this way the bullets went over the

Ball's Nieuport 16 Scout A134, in which he claimed two victories during his time with No 11 Sqn. On 2 July 1916 he was credited with a Roland C II and an Aviatik whilst flying this aircraft. The next day he used the fighter to attack a balloon with Le Prieur rockets, but did not succeed in 'flaming' it (*Bruce/Leslie collection*)

propeller blades and ended up at a pre-arranged distance. Perhaps the earliest successful aeroplane to use this latter gun arrangement was the Nieuport Scout.

The Nieuport biplane was an early design, and looked very much like an aeroplane of World War 1 should do. That is, a fuselage, an engine 'up front', two wings and a tailplane of elevator and rudder. All landplanes of that war had fixed wheels and a tail-skid. What was perhaps a little out of the ordinary was the lower wing. This was very much smaller, being narrower than other types which followed, and as such was known as the sesquiplane wing set-up – one and a half wings!

The Type was designed by one of the greatest of France's aviation pioneers, Edouard de Niéport, although for his aviation work he adopted the more familiar name of Nieuport. He began designing aircraft in 1905, but his biplane designs came later. The French naturally began to use the type, both a single (Type 10 and 11) and a two-seater (12) design, and soon the single-seater Type 10, and the 12, were taken up by the British RNAS. Despite what has been written before, the RFC did not have the Nieuport 11. The RNAS put in an order for the Type 16, which resembled the 11, but then diverted them to the RFC in March 1916.

At this early period, the Nieuports were, like other 'scouts', distributed to squadrons of mixed reconnaissance aeroplanes for both scouting and protection duties. One of these units was No 11 Sqn, but as further supplies of the new machine became available, it became possible to equip No 60 Sqn almost totally with the Type 16. Albert Ball, who as we read earlier became an exponent of the Nieuport, first flew a Type 16 on 15 May 1916 with No 11 Sqn.

ARMAMENT

The gun platform of the British Nieuport Scouts, the wing-mounted Lewis gun, was the invention of a No 11 Sqn sergeant by the name of R G Foster. Thus, the ingenious Foster Mounting embodied a quadrantal slide which permitted the gun to be slid down rearwards for changing the drum of ammunition. It did not take long for the equally inventive pilots to see that the gun could also be fired upwards once the gun was slid back, adding another dimension to their air fighting activities. It was not difficult for a good pilot to edge up beneath an opponent, whose first intimation of danger was when bullets began to slash into the underside of his aeroplane. A variety of somewhat different over-wing mounts were seen on French Nieuport 10s, 11s and 17s, the first being designed by a Sgt Moreau.

Later on, some RFC machines also used the French Alkan design mounting of a Vickers gun on the fuselage in front of the cockpit once the synchronised gun system was invented. While the French used this arrangement almost exclusively, the RFC and RNAS generally employed the wing-mounted Lewis gun, carrying a 47-round removable ammunition drum.

The most widely used variant of the Nieuport was the Type 17 (17C.1). This too was a sesquiplane configuration with the famous 'V' struts between the wings. They arrived on RFC squadrons in mid-July 1916 at the time of the Battle of the Somme, and again the first examples came via the RNAS. By the autumn the RFC had ordered many more.

BRITISH ACES

One of the early RFC aces with the Nieuport Scout was A D Bell-Irving. A Canadian from Vancouver, Duncan Bell-Irving gained his first confirmed victory on his 22nd birthday, 28 August 1916, flying a Morane with No 60 Sqn, just before the unit began to receive Nieuport Scouts. During the next two months, now flying a Nieuport (A203), he added five more scalps to his tally, including a balloon, and received the Military Cross (MC) and Bar. Wounded in combat on 9 November, Bell-Irving did not see further action, but later commanded the School of Special Flying at Gosport, in England.

Another Nieuport ace who started his scoring in 1916 was Lt E S T Cole, also of No 60 Sqn. Flying A174, he made his first claim (a Roland C II) on 15 September 1916. He was later posted to No 1 Sqn where, in 1917, he brought his score to eight, including two balloons, and won the MC. Ed Cole came from Bristol, and was 21 when he became an ace.

No 60 Sqn produced a number of successful pilots, not least of whom was the South African, Henry 'Duke' Meintjes. In the last weeks of 1916 he claimed two victories, including one Albatros two-seater forced down inside British lines on 11 December, shared with five other pilots. By the time No 60 Sqn changed to Royal Aircraft Factory SE 5a machines, 'Duke' had received the MC and scored four victories – his final war total was eight. One of the pilots he shared the 'captured' Albatros with was Lt Keith L Caldwell, from Wellington, New Zealand. This too was his second victory, although his first with a Nieuport Scout. With No 60 Sqn in 1917, Caldwell would bring his score to eight before the SE 5s came, and later, as CO of No 74 Sqn, he increased his tally to 25 by war's end. He received the MC, DFC and Bar and the Belgian *Croix de Guerre*.

By far the most productive and aggressive of the 1916 RFC air fighters was the amazing Albert Ball, who flew Nieuports with Nos 11 and 60 Sqns. This was still very much the era of the lone wolf pilots, those who could and did operate largely alone. By the very nature of the air war, aircraft invariably flew on their own for all sorts of work, or at least sortied in small formations of no more than half a dozen. Therefore, those scout pilots who were able to look after themselves could roam at will, and endeavour to engage any hostile aircraft they encountered.

This happened on both sides, with the Fokker Eindecker pilots such as Boelcke and Immelmann doing just this, although Boelcke had recognised the advantage of operating in twos or three, but only as aircraft numbers permitted. His dream of fighting units comprised of anywhere up to a dozen single-seaters was still some months away, but these two early aces, together with men such as Kurt Wintgens, Gustav Leffers and Otto Parschau were effective fighting alone against either British or French aeroplanes.

With the RFC, just like the Germans, fighting aircraft were still only scattered around in small numbers, so men like Ball, who survived for some time in air combat, managed to hone their skills. Obviously good eyesight and an appreciation of their own developing tactics helped.

Immelmann, with his ability to reverse his direction of attack, had an advantage, while Ball's ability to stalk opponents and get up underneath them before being seen, made for success.

Flying with No 11 Sqn, which operated Bristol Scouts, Nieuports and later FE 2b 'pusher' two-seaters, Ball, and his fellow pilots, tried hard to support RFC aircraft spotting for the artillery or photographing enemy strong-points and supply dumps. Having gained 11 successes by mid-August, Ball went to No 60 Sqn at Filescamp Farm. He had made his last four claims in A201, and he took this machine with him to his new unit, where he used it to raise his tally to 17 by the end of that month. Roland two-seat fighters were his main opponents during this period, but in September the first German single-seat biplanes started to make an appearance.

These new types, such as the Fokker D I and D II, the Halberstadt D II and also the new Albatros D I and D II, were beginning to equip the new *Jagdstaffeln – Jastas*. The brain-child of Oswald Boelcke, the first *Jastas* were formed in the summer of 1916 and began operating at the front from August. These were really the first dedicated German fighter units of note, although the pilots and aircraft were few. The size of a *Jasta* was smaller than that of an ordinary British or French squadron, falling generally between six to a dozen pilots. Aircraft could still be mixed at this early stage, some Fokker, Halberstadt or Albatros biplanes, but they each had a similar performance, and each *Jasta* took what it was given in an attempt to raise their unit strength to a reasonable number of men and machines.

By the very developing nature of the air war thus far, the Germans, being almost always less in number than their British and French adversaries, were forced to adopt a more defensive posture, which as month followed month, took on a more permanent look. As time progressed it seemed a good position to be in for several reasons. The pilots, staying well behind their own frontlines, could generally choose when and if to attack hostile aeroplanes. If they got themselves into a tight spot they could dive away and, if necessary, land. More often than not – although it was not guaranteed by any means – the gentlemen of the RFC would not come down and shoot them up on the ground. If they had not been wounded, or their aircraft not even seriously damaged, they could later take off and either go home or resume their task. And if they were wounded or damaged, at least they were behind friendly lines.

Only the occasional foray was made into Allied air space if the need arose to attack the balloon lines, or very occasionally an experienced 'ace' might make a fighting visit over the lines to attack some unsuspecting pilot flying along feeling secure by being so far back. Even some experienced British airmen were picked off in this way.

With a mainly prevailing west to east wind, the Allied pilots had the disadvantage of being blown into enemy territory and then had the task of battling their way back, perhaps after combat, with reduced ammunition and petrol starting to run low. As the experience of the *Jasta* pilots grew, they knew that this was a good moment to engage the RFC, whose pilots would be less aggressive if they needed to re-cross the lines soon.

The RFC, under Hugh Trenchard, had been given the task of being aggressive at all times, always taking the war to the Germans inside their own lines. It was something that was instilled into them, and it became second nature. It was to cost them dear in both men and machines, as any damage or wound might quickly bring them down to be taken prisoner. And with an improving and aggressive *Jasta* organisation, whose pilots were encouraged through decorations and high honours to increase their victory scores, life was short, even if heroic, for the young men from Britain and her Colonies.

Albert Ball continued his mercurial rise. He was a loner on the ground as well as in the air, but of course he was still only 20 years of age in the summer of 1916. Yet he continued to do his duty as he saw it, and during September brought his score to 31 – 11 of his last 12 victories were made in Nieuport A213. Most of his final claims were against Roland and Alba-tros two-seaters, whose crews were mostly trying to observe movements inside British lines. By the time he left for England, he had been awarded the MC, followed by the DSO and Bar, with a second Bar in the pipeline.

A213 was a Type 17, which was fast becoming the best of the Nieuport Scouts produced so far. Some of the initial Type 17s came fitted with a 'hemispherical fairing' fixed to the crankshaft – in reality a nose-cone (*cône de pénétration*). It remained stationary, which meant it did not turn with the propeller. However, it was soon discarded and Ball himself took his home to England one leave, and was photographed with it in the garden of his parent's house. For some years it hung in the hall of the house.

The first Type 17s began to arrive at the front in July 1916. The RFC ordered more, and by the end of the year close to 40 had been delivered. Some problems occurred with the lower wings, but by and large the pilots liked them, and they were more than a match for the opposing *Jasta* equipment. In the Spring of 1917, Nieuport 17s continued to be delivered along with some of the new Type 23s. There was little visual difference between the two types, and this being the case, record keeping on squadrons tended to confuse the two, so that it is difficult to ascertain today whether a certain machine was a Type 17 or a 23.

ROYAL NAVAL AIR SERVICE

Units of the RNAS – which had first accepted Nieuport single-seaters on the British side – did not have the scope of service or equipment to make massive inroads into the combat air war. Nevertheless, as the war continued, the RNAS gradually formed or re-equipped several fighting squadrons with frontline scouts, and supported the RFC on the Western Front.

However, only 6 Naval Squadron became fully equipped with Nieuports, supporting the RFC in the spring of 1917, and claiming a number of victories in the process. The RNAS's only ace was 23-year old Flt Lt E W Norton, who had gained his first victory with No 1 Naval Wing in a Nieuport (3994) the previous October – a balloon destroyed with the use of Le Prieur rockets, for which he won the DSC. He scored his first kill with 6 Naval on 8 February 1917, and by the end of April he had claimed a total of nine victories (one in N3184, four in N3187 and three in N3208). Later in the war Norton became a squadron commander.

Mentioning No 1 Naval Wing, we can record a possible ace with this unit – Canadian Redford Henry Mulock. 'Red' Mulock was approaching 30 years of age at the time of his combat successes, and had transferred into the RNAS from the artillery in 1915. His five 'victories' were comprised of four 'out of control' claims and one 'forced to land' between December 1915 and May 1916. He won the DSO for his work against aircraft and enemy shipping. Mulock later commanded No 3 Naval Squadron, which was one of the RNAS's best fighter units, and he ended the war as a colonel, with a Bar to his DSO.

Another pilot who later achieved 'acedom' was Australian, S J Goble DSC. Stan Goble had also joined the RNAS in 1915, and flying with 1 Naval Wing, scored two victories. He ended the war with ten, the last two as an observer in a DH 4 from 5 Naval/No 205 Sqn RAF, which he commanded. Goble later became a leading light in the postwar Royal Australian Air Force (RAAF)

SPRING 1917

Several things were happening in France in the spring of 1917. Both warring sides were planning offensives, and for their part, the German *Jastas* were just itching to get to grips with the RFC. They had grown in confidence over the autumn and winter months of 1916-17, honed their new skills, worked out their tactics and had, in the main, settled on the best of the aeroplanes available. Mostly, this was the Albatros D II and coming D III, although Halberstadt Scouts continued to be used to make up the numbers.

On the British side, there were now four squadrons fully equipped with the Nieuport Scout, namely No's 1, 29, 40 and 60 Sqns (No 11 Sqn had started to re-equip with FE 2s), and with the RNAS, just No 6 Naval Squadron, based at Petite Synthe, which was one of the many airfields around Dunkirk. 6 Naval operated along the North Sea coast, affording protection for naval bombing aircraft, although they too occasionally came further south to support the RFC.

During this spring 1917 period, while Flt Lt Norton was achieving his success with 6 Naval, the squadron gained over a dozen victories. Among the scorers were three pilots who would later become aces on other types – Flt Sub Lt R R Winter and Flt Lt B P H de Roeper, who had both gained the first of their five victories flying a Nieuport, and Squadron Commander Chris Draper.

Chris Draper DSC became famous as the 'Mad Major', for in his later life he found renewed fame by flying an Auster under several Thames bridges in 1953, aged 61. Commanding 6 Naval, he claimed two victories on 6 June 1917, although he was shot-up himself in a fight with *Jasta* 5. With the already mentioned difficulties over confirmations of claims, Draper's opponent that day was Ltn Werner Voss (see *Osprey Aircraft of the Aces 32 - Albatros Aces of World War 1* for further details), who had shot down one 6 Naval Nieuport – the German's 34th victory – before Draper gave him a slight wound and forced him to crash-land his Albatros D III. In all, Draper claimed nine victories in the war, mainly on No 3 Wing Sopwith two-seaters and later Sopwith Camels, commanding 8 Naval/No 208 Sqn RAF.

As 1917 progressed, so improved Nieuports became available. The Types 23 and 27 began to appear, and the British squadrons might have a combination of these, plus the 17 on strength. However, the 17s tended to be replaced as more of the 27s were taken on strength. Those French

Pilots of No 1 Sqn pose together in July 1917. They are, from left to right, Capt P Fullard and Lts H G Reeves, W W Rogers, J B Maudsley, H S Preston, T T Gibbon (RO) and C S I Lavers, sat astride the shoulders of F M McLaren. These pilots were credited with a total of 67 victories (*Bruce/Leslie collection*)

Lt W C Campbell (23 victories) is seen seated in Nieuport Scout B3474 which carries the individual marking '2', repeated on the fuselage decking. Note the red stripes painted on the cowling and the absence of a vertical red line, which then served as the squadron marking, aft of the fuselage cockade (*Bruce/Leslie collection*)

escadrilles still operating with Nieuports also tended to equip with the 27s.

However, during the summer of 1917 it was clear the Nieuports were being outclassed by the German *Jastas*, and SE 5a fighters began to re-equip the RFC units. No 60 Sqn re-equipped in July 1917 and No 40 Sqn in October, while Nos 1 and 29 Sqns soldiered on until the spring of 1918, when they too finally switched to the SE 5a in March and April respectively.

No 1 Sqn

The Nieuport Scout pilots of No 1 Sqn held a phenomenal combat record during 1917-18. Like other units, it initially had a variety of aircraft types – Bristol Scouts, Moranes of various denominations, two-seater Nieuport 10s and even the odd Martinsyde. However, the arrival of the Nieuport 16 in March 1916 began the period of dedicated fighting duties, and by the end of that year No 1 Sqn was fully equipped with Nieuport Scouts. This finally led to it being officially designated a scout unit in February 1917, by which time it had standardised on Nieuport 17s.

Commanded by Maj Guy C StP de Dombasle from December 1916 to June 1917, it had already achieved some fame in air fighting with around 20 'victories'. The unit had been based at Bailleul since March 1915, and continued to operate from here for all of its Nieuport days. Most World War 1 fighter squadrons had a number of their pilots emerge as high-scoring aces, but No 1 Sqn was exceptional even at this stage, and most of its scorers in 1917 were, or became, aces – or achieved ace status with other units.

One pilot who quickly rose to be a flight commander on the squadron, and a future Knight and Air Vice Marshal, was C J Quintin-Brand. Christopher Quintin-Brand was a South African, and he claimed his first seven victories with No 1 Sqn between March and May 1917. He received the MC and scored all his successes in A6668, including one two-seater forced down inside British lines. Quintin-Brand later became an ace twice-over as a nightfighter pilot, commanding No 151 Sqn (Camels) in 1918.

Among the bevy of up-and-coming aces, three names stand out during the first half of 1917, Hazell, Fullard and Campbell. Tom Falcon Hazell, aged 25, came from Galway, Ireland, although he'd been educated at Tonbridge School, in Kent. Like so many World War 1 flyers, he had transferred into the RFC via the army, in his case the 7th Battalion, Royal Inniskilling Fusiliers. Many of these men had not only served with the army but seen action in France early in the war, and so had Tom Hazell.

Once with No 1 Sqn, he took some time to find his 'aerial feet', but his first claim came on 4 March 1917 in Nieuport A6604. A second victory followed in April and a third in May. Having survived thus far was often an achievement. The oft-used phrase that pilots in World War 1 survived on the Western Front only three weeks, may have been worked out as some kind of average, but in reality this is just journalistic convenience, used to shock. Pilots often survived long periods on frontline squadrons, whilst others did not survive their first patrols, but many, like Hazell, managed to live long enough to learn their trade – a trade, in any event, still basically new to the world. There were no text books on how to do it, and fewer too were the men to ask who had achieved success in aerial combat.

Campbell's B3474, seen closest to the camera in this autumn 1917 photograph, is now marked with the red line. Next to it is Wendell Rogers' B3629 (*Bruce/Leslie collection*)

However, as June arrived so Hazell's scoring began to increase, as if finally 'getting his eye in', things jelled. Six further victories in the first nine days of the month were followed by five in July – a double on the 12th, a triple on the 22nd. Six victories in August brought his score to 20 (ten destroyed, ten 'out of control'), all on Nieuports (six flying B1649 and the last 11 in B3455). He had won the MC and become a flight commander. In his next tour as a flight commander in No 24 Sqn flying SE 5s, Hazell would raise his score to 43, for which he received the DSO, DFC and Bar, and was granted a permanent commission in the RAF.

If Tom Hazell had been good, then Philip Fletcher Fullard was exceptional. Born north of London in June 1897, he was only 24 when his prowess as an air fighter became supreme. Serving with the Royal Fusiliers, he by-passed the usual channels by learning to fly at his own expense, before transferring to the RFC. Completing his training via the Central Flying School, Fullard was obviously an above average pilot for he was retained as an instructor at the end of 1916. However, he eventually got to France in late April, and by the end of May had two claims, both in B1599.

In June and July 1917 Fullard raised his score to 15, although only four of these are recorded as destroyed. His first claim in August was a two-seater he shared with another pilot, which they forced down inside British lines – it has to be said that No 1 Sqn tended to share victories more readily than some other units. While this does not really detract from the pilots' achievements, it did tend to make higher scores for them. To clarify this, if four pilots shared a claim, each man received an acknowledged victory, even though only one German aircraft had gone down. The French also used this system, although as already mentioned, the Germans did not. If more than one German

Nieuport Scout A6603 was flown by Lt E S T Cole of No 1 Sqn. He claimed two of his eight Nieuport victories in this machine in March and April 1917 (*via M O'Connor*)

Capt T F Hazell in his No 1 Sqn Nieuport (either B1649 or B3455). Note that the red cowling stripes look a little worn (*via Hazell family*)

pilot claimed the same kill, one or other of them would credit the other, or where there was a dispute, generally between pilots of different *Jastas*, the claim went to arbitration, and without recourse was given to one of the claimants.

Fullard, by now a captain and flight commander, continued claiming throughout August (12 victories), had a rest in September, but in October gained a further 11 kills. With his final two successes in mid-November, this brought his total to 40 – all on Nieuports – and thus he became the highest scoring Nieuport pilot in the RFC. By this time he had received the DSO and the MC and Bar.

Two days after his 40th victory, on 17 November 1917, Fullard broke a leg in a football match, which, being slow to heal, effectively put him out of the war. One has to wonder what sort of total victories he may have achieved had he continued in action or, after a rest (which was due), returned to France with another unit. Of course, the luck of this game also meant he might well have been killed on his very next sortie, but Fullard had certainly found his form, and knew what he was doing in the dangerous skies over France.

Lt William Charles Campbell was the third of No 1 Sqn's high-scoring trio, born in Bordeaux, France, of a Scottish father and a French mother, in April 1889. The oldest of the three pilots, he was 28 at the time of his greatest success. Campbell joined the RFC in 1916, and arrived at No 1 Sqn on the first day of May 1917. It took him just two weeks to down his first German aeroplane, a two-seater over Polygon Wood on 14 May, and his second, a kite balloon, was claimed five days later. During June he brought his score to 14 flying mostly B1700, and in July, using B3466 and B3474, and now a flight commander, Campbell increased his tally to 23 – four of these were balloons. He was wounded on the last day of that

Capt Tom Falcon Hazell of No 1 Sqn in 1917. No fewer than 20 of his eventual 43 victories were scored flying Nieuport Scouts (*via Hazell family*)

month. His various successes against balloons brought his total of 'gas bags' to five, which made him the first RFC balloon ace of the war.

Campbell's wounding came on the first day of the Battle of Ypres. At the time he was flying B3474 on a special mission – in light of his recent experience, he had probably been sent out to attack and force down German observation balloons. Engaged by German fighters, his Nieuport was shot-up and he was wounded in the thigh, probably by Obltn Eduard von Dostler of *Jasta* 6. Von Dostler, leader of *Jasta*

This photograph of Capt W W Rogers in his No 1 Sqn Nieuport clearly shows the fighter's Aldis sight, windscreen, Lewis gun and Bowden cable

No 1 Sqn's Capt Rogers and B6789 sit in the snow in December 1917. He claimed three kills in this machine, and it was also used by fellow ace Philip Fullard

Capt Philip Fullard of No 1 Sqn, who was the ranking RFC Nieuport ace of World War 1 with 40 kills

6, claimed a Nieuport Scout down on the British side west of Bellewarde at 1405 German time, Campbell's loss being recorded at 1305 British time. German time at this stage was one hour ahead of British time.

Campbell had won the MC and Bar for his prowess, to which he added the DSO in September. He was lucky to have survived his meteoric career, all his claims coming in exactly three months. Other aces would do as well, but many failed to survive such an intense period of air combat.

Another No 1 Sqn ace in Campbell's flight was Frank Sharpe. He had previously served with the squadron as an observer during the time it had two-seaters, but having requested pilot training, was sent back to England. It was not always possible to return to one's earlier unit once having become a pilot, but Sharpe did, and in little over five weeks claimed five victories – three in B1500 and two in B3481. However, on 9 June he was shot down in the latter Nieuport by Obltn Kurt von Döring of *Jasta* 4, wounded and taken into captivity. A Londoner, he was 21 years old.

Although in the early years of the war there were many NCO pilots, very few became aces as such. One who did was Sgt G P Olley. Gordon Olley transferred to the RFC from the army and had, like Frank Sharpe, seen service with No 1 Sqn before taking to flying, but in his case he had been a motor cycle despatch rider. However, he was willing to fly and so became a corporal observer. Asking for pilot training, Olley too returned to No 1 Sqn with his pilot's wings, and in the summer and early autumn of 1917 achieved ten combat victories, which brought him the Military

Medal. Four of his victories were achieved in B1681 and four in B3628. Olley later became a ferry pilot, and postwar flew with KLM and then Imperial Airways.

Another exceptional pilot was Capt L F Jenkin MC and Bar. Another Londoner, this 22-year old transferred from the 9th Loyal North Lancashire Regiment and arrived on No 1 Sqn on 15 May 1917. Before the month was out he had two victory claims, and by the end of July his tally had been increased to 20. No fewer than 15 of these had been whilst flying B1547.

Sgt G P Olley of No 1 Sqn claimed ten victories. Postwar, Gordon Olley became a well known civil airline pilot (*Bruce/Leslie collection*)

Jenkin's final two victories came in September, but on the day he made his final claim, 11 September (the same day that French ace Georges Guynemer was killed), he fell to Obltn Otto Schmidt of *Jasta* 29. This was the German's eighth kill of an eventual 20. Jenkin's B3635 fell northeast of Bixschoote at 1930 German time.

Although Nieuport B6768 has been camouflaged, it still carries the red fuselage marking of No 1 Sqn. Marked with the letter 'X', this aircraft was used by Gordon Olley to claim one victory on 5 October 1917, while Lt W D Patrick (later Lord Patrick) claimed another kill on the 24th. The latter ace scored four Nieuport and three SE 5 victories in total

No 1 Sqn in fact lost two of its aces on this day, the other being Lt W S Mansell from Wimbledon, south London, who, had he lived till 25 September, would have reached his 21st birthday. William went to France with the 3rd East Surrey Regiment, prior to transferring to the RFC as an observer with No 22 Sqn. Wounded in August 1916 after gaining one kill, he then became a pilot and with No 1 Sqn and scored four more victories. On 11 September, flying B3648 (the Nieuport in which he had achieved his fifth victory two days earlier), he was shot and killed by anti-aircraft fire south of Houthem.

Robert Alexander Birkbeck, from Bournemouth, was another youngster you achieved 'acedom' with No 1 Sqn in 1917. He joined the unit on 10 June, later became a captain and by the time he left for England in February 1918, had scored ten victories. Six of these were claimed in B6753 and three in B1582. A belated DFC was awarded in 1918.

Lt E S T Cole, from Bristol, had scored his first victory flying Nieuports with No 60 Sqn in September 1916, but had then moved to No 1 Sqn. Between March and the first day of May, he brought his claims to eight, the last one being an Albatros Scout of *Jasta* 28 shot down behind British lines flying B1508. He won the MC, but did not see further action until World War 2.

Lumsden Cummings hailed from Ottawa, Canada, and he was 21 when he achieved five victories on Nieuports in 1917. He was promoted to captain shortly before leaving the unit to go into hospital on 9 February 1918. Charles Lavers, from St Albans, scored five victories in 1917 on Nieuports. He had already seen flying service as an observer (in FE 2s) with No 23 Sqn, but had been wounded in the head in November 1916. Becoming a pilot himself, Lavers arrived on No 1 Sqn on 1 June 1917. Converting to SE 5s in 1918, and following a period on a Home Defence squadron, he came back to the unit and brought his score to nine, winning the DFC.

Guy Moore was another Canadian from No 1 Sqn. A native of Vancouver, he was 22 years old when he arrived on the unit on 16 August 1917. Flying Nieuports, he scored five of his six victories in B1508 and won the MC. Promoted to captain, and flight commander, Moore flew SE 5s after conversion, but was killed on 7 April 1918 when his fighter was hit by an anti-aircraft shell and exploded. By this date he had added three more victories to his tally.

Thirteen victory claims were made by Harry Gosford Reeves from Binfield, Berkshire (although he had also lived in Taunton), between 18 June and 18 November 1917. He had joined the squadron on 10 June 1917, and it took him just eight days to down his first

Capt L F Jenkin claimed 22 Nieuport victories with No 1 Sqn prior to being killed in action on 11 September 1917

Capt G B Moore of No 1 Sqn is seen seated in B1508. He used this fighter to claim five of his seven Nieuport victories, the remaining two being scored in B3639. Moore was killed in action 7 April 1918 when his SE 5 suffered a direct hit from an AA shell (*Bruce/Leslie collection*)

Capt W V T Rooper achieved eight victories with No 1 Sqn prior to being shot down and killed by German ace Ltn Xaver Dannhuber of *Jasta* 26 on 9 October 1917

opponent in B1650. Five of his victories came in B1672 and his last four in B6774. Promoted to flight commander in the autumn, Reeves was killed in a flying accident at Bailleul on 24 January 1918.

The smiling face of William Wendell Rogers, a native of Alberton, on Prince Edward Island in Canada, adorns many book and articles on World War 1 aviators. He is seen seated in his No 1 Sqn Nieuport Scout, giving the world then, and now, a portrait of what people think World War 1 fighter aces looked like. And an ace he was, scoring nine victories in the second half of 1917 and winning the MC. Of his claims, all were of the 'out of control' variety except one, and this, unusually, was a huge Gotha bomber which he shot down on 12 December north of Frelinghein at 1415 in the afternoon, flying B6825. This machine, from *Bogohl* 3, had been intercepted during one of the Gotha's rare daylight raids over France. Its pilot had been Hauptmann Rudolf Kleine, who died along with his three crewmen.

Kleine was quite a famous German airman, having been decorated with the *Pour le Mèrite* two months earlier, and had made several bombing raids against London. Rogers commanded 'C' Flight, and three of his victories were in B6789.

Capt W V T Rooper, from Denbigh, also joined No 1 Sqn in the early summer of 1917 following service with the Welsh Fusiliers, and by mid-September was a flight commander. Claiming eight victories, four in B6767 and three in B1675, he received the Belgian *Croix de Guerre*. He was shot down by Ltn Xaver Dannhuber of *Jasta* 26 on 9 October, becoming the German's seventh victory.

Among the other notable pilots of No 1 Sqn were a number who began their fighting careers with the unit and achieved 'acedom' either on SE 5s, or with other units altogether. Among them were Capt C C Clark from Norwich. He scored three Nieuport victories in March 1917, but returned to the squadron in 1918 and brought his score to ten before being taken prisoner.

Capt H J Hamilton, from London, gained his first success with No 1 Sqn, then moved to No 29 Sqn towards the end of 1917 as a flight commander. Serving with the latter unit, he downed two hostile aircraft and then returned to No 1 Sqn during its SE 5 period. He scored a further three victories, taking his final tally to six overall.

Capt James Douglas Latta MC, from London, had began operational flying as a two-seater pilot, but by early 1916 had been moved to No 1 Sqn. In June he claimed three victories, but in October went to No 60 Sqn as a flight commander. Latta shot down two German aircraft in A135 to become a Nieuport ace. In 1917, flying Pups with No 66 Sqn, he was wounded by a pilot from *Jasta* 8 and saw no further combat.

Two of Latta's early victories had been against balloons, No 1 Sqn having made concentrated attacks upon the German balloon lines on

Lts H J Hamilton and H G Reeves of No 1 Sqn pose in full flying gear by Nieuport B6774

25 and 26 June with rockets. The unit had destroyed five in all, with one being credited to future No 56 Sqn CO, Capt R Balcombe-Brown.

Welshman Leslie Mansbridge claimed four victories with No 1 Sqn in 1917 but had to wait until he was a flight commander with No 23 Sqn, flying Sopwith Dolphins, to get his fifth. Mansbridge had been wounded on 3 June 1917, in B1639, by a German Marine pilot.

Capt W D Patrick, a Scot from Ayrshire, got to No 1 Sqn in September 1917 and claimed four victories in Nieuports (three in B6830). Promoted to flight commander, he then flew SE 5s in 1918 and increased his score to seven before being shot down and taken prisoner on 10 April.

Last, but by no means least, James A Slater, who was to end the war with 24 combat victories, cut his teeth with No 1 Sqn, although he had also been an observer with No 18 Sqn. His first two successes were made during February and March 1917, but he made his name with No 64 Sqn winning the MC and Bar, then the DFC.

A later view of now Capt H J Hamilton, taken whilst serving with No 29 Sqn as a flight commander

MARKINGS

Quite often the RFC Nieuports retained the silver-doping the French used, although others were camouflaged, some in the French fashion, or in the standard British khaki-green. Where the original French doping was retained, the squadron identification marking of a vertical line painted just behind the fuselage roundel was in black or red. On 'dark' aircraft this could be in white too. At first there appears to have been no use of individual aircraft markings. However, in the early summer of 1917 numbers began to be used (white, edged in black), which were later changed to single letters. These markings took the form of a red or black letter, repeated on the top starboard wing.

Photographs show that the fuselage numbers were sometimes applied ahead of the fuselage roundel, and sometimes behind it. Letters between 'A' and 'S' (but not including 'I') were normally used, although one photograph does exist showing an aircraft with the letter 'X'. Therefore, at times other letters between 'T' and 'Z' may have been used too.

Finally, in the famous picture of Nieuports lined up in the snow at Bailleul, the vertical red stripe is repeated on the fuselage decking 'fore and aft'. The squadron changed to SE 5as in March/April 1918.

NO 29 SQN

This unit was formed at Gosport in November 1915 and equipped with Airco DH 2 scouts. Going to France in March 1916, it operated these 'pusher' machines for a year, re-equipping with Nieuports in March 1917. For most of 1916 it had been at Abeele, but it was at Le Hameau when the Nieuports arrived, its CO being Maj H V Champion de Crespigny MC.

In July 1917 its CO was Maj C M B Chapman MC, who had gained three confirmed kills with No 24 Sqn. Becoming a flight commander with No 29 Sqn, he 'made ace' on 4 June 1917 by downing a *Jasta* 11 pilot inside British lines. Having increased his score to seven, and been given command of No 29 Sqn, Chapman was killed by bomb fragments during an air raid on the unit's base at Poperinghe on 1 October. His brother, an observer with No 22 Sqn, was killed in action on 7 October. Following Chapman came Maj C H Dixon, who led No 29 Sqn until early 1919.

Capt J G Coombe came to the squadron in October 1917. A former observer, he became a flight commander just before he left the unit as the SE 5s began to arrive, having achieved seven victories over the winter months.

Capt C W Cudemore gained five victories flying Nieuports – two with No 40 Sqn in May 1917, then three more with No 29 Sqn during the summer. Essex-born Charles Cudemore went on to become a flight commander with No 64 Sqn (flying SE 5s) in 1918, raised his score to 15 and won the DFC.

Philip August de Fontenay came from his home in Mauritius, and prior to joining the RFC had served with the French Foreign Legion. After a very brief stay with No 40 Sqn, he transferred to No 29 Sqn and gained five victories between September 1917 and January 1918.

Capt H J Hamilton, as mentioned previously, gained six victories during the war, three on Nieuports (one with No 1 Sqn and two with No 29 Sqn), before returning to No 1 Sqn in 1918 to add his final three. He died flying a Sopwith Camel in Yorkshire in June 1918.

Lt D'Arcy Fowlis Hilton, an American from Michigan (although born in Toronto, Canada) not only scored eight victories with No 29 Sqn, but achieved six of them in Nieuport B3494 – a machine like so many others, that was later sent to the Middle East. Awarded the MC, he spent the rest of the war as an instructor in England and in Canada, for which he received the AFC. Hilton's son was killed flying in World War 2, and he himself died shortly after the end of that conflict.

Capt A G Jones-Williams flew alongside Hilton in 1917, having joined No 29 Sqn in March 1917. Promoted to flight commander in May, he was awarded the MC and a Bar in July. With eight victories he was rested, returning to France in 1918 to fly Camels with No 65 Sqn, bringing his score to 11. As a squadron leader in the postwar RAF, Jones-Williams died in a crash during a non-stop attempt to fly from England to South Africa on 17 December 1929. Earlier in the year he had flown non-stop from Cranwell to India in a Fairey Monoplane.

Capt Earl Stanley Meek came from Ontario, Canada, and arrived at No 29 Sqn on 14 July 1917. Before the month was out he had downed his

This camouflaged No 29 Sqn Nieuport Scout (B3578) was being flown by Lt P A De Fontenay when he shot down an Albatros two-seater on 12 November 1917. The fighter was itself lost just 15 days later, its pilot, Lt L Kert, becoming a prisoner of war (*via M O'Connor*)

Lt Philip De Fontenay, from Mauritius, scored five victories with No 29 Sqn in 1917 (*via M O'Connor*)

Nieuport 23 B3494 was flown by American Lt D'Arcy F Hilton of No 29 Sqn, who used it to score six of his eight victories. This photo was taken in Palestine in 1918, where many Western Front Nieuports ended up (*Bruce/Leslie collection*)

Lt D F Hilton, at the rear, poses with other pilots from No 29 Sqn. They are, from left to right, Capt A G Jones-Williams (eight Nieuport victories, plus three more on Camels with No 65 Sqn in 1918), and Lts Fenwick and C W Cudemore, the latter of whom scored five Nieuport victories with Nos 40 and 29 Sqns and a further ten on SE 5s with No 64 Sqn in 1918 (*via M O'Connor*)

first enemy aircraft, but it was December before he scored again. However, by the end of January 1918, having been promoted to flight commander, he had achieved six victories, one being shared with Philip August de Fontenay. After the war he became a school teacher.

Lt A W B Miller had been an observer with No 1 Sqn before becoming a pilot. Coming to No 29 Sqn in May 1917, he gained six victories during June and July, all whilst flying B1506 '6C'. The 20-year-old was killed in combat on 13 July, shot down by German ace Ltn Hans Adam of *Jasta* 6, the latter's fifth victory.

Capt E W Molesworth MC came to No 29 Sqn from No 60 Sqn, where he had already achieved six victories, two of them on SE 5s. Whilst with the former unit he added a further twelve Nieuport victories, ten of them in B6812. Molesworth received a Bar to his MC and also the Italian Medal for Military Valour.

Capt T A Oliver had gained two victories with No 1 Sqn (one on a Nieuport) then became an ace with No 29 Sqn on 12 August 1917 as a flight commander. He was shot down and killed in combat with Obltn Ernst Wiegand of *Jasta* 10 on 14 August.

Capt J D Payne initially learnt to fly as an NCO, and his first posting was to No 41 Sqn, but he soon moved to No 29 Sqn in August. Just six days later he downed his first German machine. During the autumn Payne became a flight commander, won the MC and by early 1918 had gained 14 victories. After the war he flew as a barnstormer, and later lived in Belgium.

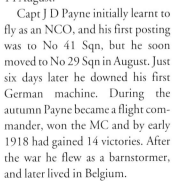

Capt T A Oliver claimed two victories with No 1 Sqn and three with No 29 Sqn between 1916 and his death in combat with *Jasta* 10 on 14 August 1917

Capt R H Rusby cut his combat teeth with Nieuports, gaining three victories over the winter of 1917-18, then went on to score a total of ten kills by the end of May, on SE 5s. The Londoner also received the DFC.

Capt A S Shepherd hailed from New South Wales, Australia. Transferring from the Australian Army into the RFC, he joined No 29 Sqn towards the end of 'Bloody April'. In just over two months he had claimed ten victories and won the MC. Shepherd was made 'C' Flight commander, and then came the award of the DSO, but on 20 July he was shot down and killed during a fight with *Jasta* 11, falling to Ltn Alfred Niederhoff. He was the German's sixth victory. Nine of Shepherd's kills were scored in B1504 'IC', the machine in which he was to lose his life.

Lt Francis Jefferies Williams was posted to No 29 Sqn on 4 September 1917, and by March of the following year he had achieved five victories.

Walter Bertram Wood scored 13 Nieuport victories in just two-and-a-half months. From Grimsby, born in October 1898, his 'war' started as a Boy Scout coast-watcher until he was old enough to enlist. Commissioned into an army regiment, Wood then transferred to the RFC, and in March 1917 was posted to No 29 Sqn. He did not score until 11 May, and then not again until 2 June, but by the end of July had a tally of 12 victories and the MC. He gained his 13th kill on 9 August on a joy-ride prior to his leaving for England. Awarded a Bar to his MC, Wood went to a Home Defence unit and was

Capt J D Payne achieved 14 victories with No 29 Sqn between August 1917 and January 1918 (*via M O'Connor*)

Lt W B Wood claimed all 13 of his victories whilst flying with No 29 Sqn between May and August 1917. Having survived a long spell in the frontline, he was killed when his Home Defence Camel crashed during a routine flight in England on 11 November 1917 – ten days after his 19th birthday!

A line up of No 29 Sqn Nieuport 17s, possibly at Le Hameau, in the early summer of 1917. These aircraft all carry the squadron marking of a large red band around the rear fuselage. The scouts are from C Flight, as noted by the codes suffixed 'C', and include A6788 '5C', A6787 '3C', B1504 '1C' (flown by ten-kill ace Capt A S Shepherd) and B1506 '6C' (Lt A W B Miller's machine in which he scored all six of his victories). The last two machines in this line up may be B1665 and A6657 (*Bruce/Leslie collection*)

killed in a Camel crash just ten days after his 19th birthday, on 11 November 1917.

MARKINGS

The No 29 Sqn's identification marking was a broad red band round the fuselage, about two-thirds back from the cockpit. Individual markings were by flights, with a large letter ('A', 'B' or 'C') beneath the cockpit rim and a large number – '1C', '2C', '3C' etc. In the early summer of 1917 for example, Shepherd as flight commander flew '1C', whilst Miller flew '6C'. Generally, the Nieuports were silver-doped, although the upper surfaces of wings and fuselage appear camouflaged khaki-green in some photographs. Different colouring on the wheel discs also differentiated the flights.

When the machines were camouflaged the marking was changed to two white vertical bands on either side of the fuselage roundel. However, during this transition period, it may be that some machines carried no squadron marking – for example, de Fontenay's Nieuport in November carried just a letter 'B' below the cockpit, repeated on the top starboard wing. No 29 Sqn re-equipped with SE 5as during April 1918.

No 40 SQN

This was another former 'pusher' squadron, although the unit has flown the FE 8 rather than the DH 2. No 40 Sqn was formed at Gosport in February 1916 and went to France during August. By the time it re-equipped with Nieuports in March 1917, its CO was Maj L A Tilney MC, who would command it until his death in action in March 1918 – by which time the squadron was flying SE 5s, which it began to receive in October 1917. The unit was at Treziennes at the time of the Nieuports' arrival, then operated from Auchel for most of its days with the French fighter.

Lt J L Barlow was born in January 1899, so was only 18 at the time of his combat days with No 40 Sqn. His first two victories were claimed on 9 June during a lone sortie to the German balloon lines. Seeing a formation of two-seaters and scouts, he attacked and shot down one of each. Two more victories came in July and two more in August, but Barlow was then killed in a flying accident in B1670 – the machine in which he had scored his last three kills. He received a Mention in Despatches.

Capt W A 'Bill' Bond DSO MC and Bar was ten years older than John Barlow, and a married man. Anyone who has read the book written by his wife Aimee following his death in action (*An Airman's Wife*, Herbert Jenkins Ltd, 1918) will learn a good deal about this man. He joined No 40 Sqn in early 1917, and within a month – from 10 May to 9 June – had claimed five German aircraft whilst flying B1545. However, on 22 June he was killed in action, either by fire from a German two-seater or, as his pals recorded, a direct hit by AA fire.

These four pilots from No 40 Sqn are, from left to right, Lts H B Redler (three of his ten victories claimed on Nieuports), R N Hall (five victories) and E L Bath, and Capt W A Bond (five victories), who was killed in action on 22 July 1917

Lt H E O Ellis of No 40 Sqn claimed seven victories, including the rare feat of three in one day on 4 May 1917

Capt G B Crole, a Scot from Edinburgh, also gained five victories during the summer of 1917 – three in B1552 and two in A6793. He was awarded the MC and became a flight commander with No 43 Sqn (flying Camels) in September, but was shot down by ground fire to become a prisoner of war on 22 November. Postwar he became a solicitor in his home town.

C W Cudemore, as mentioned earlier, became an ace with No 29 Sqn, but scored his first two kills with No 40 Sqn – two balloons on 7 May, shared with Bob Hall (see below).

Lt H E O Ellis, a Londoner, had won the MC with the army prior to his RFC service. During April and May 1917 he shot down seven German machines. According to his report on 4 May, he attacked a group of three Albatros Scouts over Douai that evening. He shot down one which crashed from 500 ft, and forced another to crash-land and turn over. Engaged from behind by the other D III, Ellis ran out of ammunition, so getting beneath the German, he pulled out his Colt automatic and emptied it at his foe, whereupon the aircraft side-slipped, shed its bottom wing at 200 ft and crashed into a pond – *Jasta* 33 had a pilot mortally wounded on this day. Two days later Ellis was injured in a crash and was sent home. These last three victories were scored flying B1545.

Capt R N Hall, from South Africa, joined the RFC from the artillery. Posted to No 40 Sqn in early 1917, Bob Hall had claimed five victories by mid-August, including three balloons on 7 May, flying B1542, two of which he shared with C W Cudemore. He then returned and served with Home Defence in England.

Maj A W Keen had seen action with No 70 Sqn in 1916 on Sopwith 1$\frac{1}{2}$ Strutters, with whom he gained his first combat success. Coming to No 40 Sqn as a flight commander in the spring of 1917, he claimed 11 more victories and received the MC. Six of his victories were whilst flying B3465. After a rest Keen returned to No 40 Sqn as its Commanding Officer, and had added two more kills on SE 5s by the time he was severely injured in a crash in August 1918. He died in September.

Maj G L 'Zulu' Lloyd, as his nickname implies, came from South Africa. Like a few others, he became an ace flying with two Nieuport squadrons. Having secured four kills with No 60 Sqn, he was sent to No 40 Sqn as a flight commander, where he downed his fifth victory on 14

South African Lt R N Hall stands by his Nieuport 17, marked with the number '1' on its fuselage. With him is Aircraft Mechanic Gurney and Sgts Bone and Mather (*Bruce/Leslie collection*)

July 1917. By October, when Lloyd left the unit, his score had risen to eight, and he had received the MC. Later, in 1918, he received the AFC.

William MacLanachan joined the RFC from the army and was posted to No 40 Sqn in France in the spring of 1917. He often flew with, and was a close friend of, Mick Mannock, and he achieved seven victories – six on Nieuports, with the last of these coming after the SE 5s had begun to arrive. He did not receive any decorations, some say because he disliked his CO, and showed it. However, he gained undying fame as the author of the book *Fighter Pilot*, written under the pen name of 'McScotch'.

Edward Mannock was destined to become the British 'ace-of-aces', mainly through the good offices of his pal Ira Jones, who later flew with him in No 74 Sqn, and wrote a book about him after the war. To ensure he took top place, Jones stated that he had 73 combat successes, one more than Bishop's 72. While we know now that Mannock did not achieve such a high score, he is still regarded as one of the best of Britain's World War 1 fighter aces.

Mick Mannock was no youngster, being 27 when the war started. After getting out of Turkey, where the war found him, he joined the RAMC, commissioned into the REs and then transferred to the RFC. One of his instructors was James McCudden, who later received the VC. Sent to No 40 Sqn in April 1917, success eluded him (except for a balloon on 7 May in one of the unit's famous 'balloon strafes'), and there was even some suggestion of him not being aggressive enough. All this was not helped by becoming lost on his first patrol, then overturning on landing. Mannock also had a narrow escape on 19 April when the lower wing of his Nieuport Scout fell away over the airfield, although he managed to get down without injury.

Despite a slow start, he gradually found his feet, got his 'eye in' and started to score victories. By 25 September he had achieved 15 victories, won the MC and been promoted to flight commander. His final victory with No 40 Sqn was scored flying an SE 5 on 1 January 1918. Mannock later gained fame with No 74 Sqn, and then as CO of No 85 Sqn, before his death in action on 26 July, with a score thought to be around 61.

The following three pilots who became aces on SE 5s had each opened their scoring on Nieuports with No 40 Sqn. I P R Napier downed two before adding ten more on SEs, whilst Lt H B Redler gained his first three of ten on Nieuports – his last eight kills were with No 24 Sqn, and included the German ace Adolf von Tutschek. The last of the trio was Capt J H Tudhope, the South African scoring two of his ten victories on Nieuports, and all with No 40 Sqn. His second Nieuport claim was shared with Flight Commander C D Booker of 8 Naval Squadron, the pilot of the Albatros D V, who was captured, being Hans Waldhausen, an ace with *Jasta* 37. Both of 'Tud's' claims were whilst flying B3617. With the MC and Bar, he later served with the RCAF and died in Ontario in October 1956.

MARKINGS

No 40 Sqn Nieuports carried a white band round the fuselage forward of the roundel and two similar bands forward of the tailplane. Individual letters, in red, were placed immediately behind the roundel, ahead of the two rear white bands.

Maj A W Keen joined No 40 Sqn in the spring of 1917 as a flight commander, and claimed 11 of his 14 victories flying Nieuport Scouts. Following a period of rest, he returned to the unit in 1918 as its CO, by which time No 40 Sqn was flying SE 5s. Keen was to die on 12 September from injuries suffered in a flying accident that had occurred the previous month

Lt William MacLanachan of No 40 Sqn. One of his Nieuports was B3608, which carried the letter 'L' (in red?) on the fuselage aft of the roundel. Squadron markings were one white band behind the cockpit and two white bands round the rear fuselage. 'Mac' scored eight victories, seven on Nieuports

Flanked by groundcrewmen and fellow pilot Lt R N Hall (standing by the spinner, which was reportedly later painted yellow), Lt E 'Mick' Mannock is seen seated in his No 40 Sqn Nieuport 17, complete with wing streamers, in 1917. The groundcrewmen are, from left to right, Flt Sgt Hancock and Sgts Jackson and Mather (and two unknown airmen). Mannock scored 15 Nieuport victories between May and September 1917 (*Bruce/Leslie collection*)

No 60 Sqn

This famous World War 1 unit was formed at Gosport in April 1916 and went to France within a month, but it was not until August that it equipped with Nieuport Scouts. During the summer of 1916 and into 1917, based at various airfields, but mostly at Filescamp Farm (in 1917), the unit had several famous pilots among its personnel, not the least of whom was Maj A J L Scott MC. No 60 Sqn flew the Nieuport until they were replaced by SE 5s in July 1917.

By far the most famous pilot to fly with the unit was Albert Ball. The 20-year-old from Nottingham had already seen considerable action prior to his posting to No 60 Sqn, having flown two-seater BE 2s with No 13 Sqn. His aggressiveness in the air led to him being permitted to fly a single-seat Nieuport Scout after he moved to No 11 Sqn in May 1916. This unit had been flying the Vickers FB 5 'Gunbus', but had received Nieuports and Bristol Scouts prior to the arrival of FE 2b 'pusher' two-seaters in the summer of 1916. At that time its Nieuports went to No 60 Sqn.

However, Ball had by this time achieved 11 victories whilst generally flying lone patrols, which was the type of operation usually conducted by scouting pilots, and one which suited Ball's temperament. It was also a time when claims began to be categorised, and when a victory could mean just that - not necessarily a destroyed opponent. At this early stage a victory could be a 'moral' one just as easily as a 'material' one. An aircraft whose pilot had been forced down to land could be just as important as one crashed, for the airman had been stopped doing his job – especially important if that job was reconnaissance or artillery directing.

Ball used his flying ability to stalk his opponents, often coming up beneath them in order to fire up into the belly of the machine, using the wing-mounted Lewis gun pulled

Seen sitting between two Bristol Monoplanes in the Middle East in 1918, Nieuport B1552 had previously been flown in France by Mick Mannock during his time with No 40 Sqn (*via M O'Connor*)

down on the Foster apparatus. The latter device also allowed the gun to be pulled down to replace an empty drum of ammunition, but it could also be used to fire upwards when in this position.

During the summer of 1916, and especially during the Battle of the Somme, Ball and his brother pilots achieved much success but Ball was exceptional. Soon, he had received the MC, then the DSO and Bar. By the end of September he had amassed 31 claims in this period. After a rest Ball became a flight commander with the first SE 5 unit, No 56 Sqn, and returned to France with it in April 1917. Even then he was allowed to have his own personal Nieuport (B1522) and in this he gained his 32nd victory on 23 April.

However, the air war had changed now, and it was no longer safe for any pilot to venture about on his own. The patrol war was now in being, groups of pilots flying together under an experienced patrol leader. Ball still occasionally flew on his own, but the rest of his victories were all achieved in the SE 5. His total 'victories' reached 44 before he was killed on 7 May, becoming disoriented in cloud and coming out too low to recover before slamming into the ground. He had already received a second Bar to his DSO and then, posthumously, the Victoria Cross. And he was still only 20.

Another of the early aces was Capt Duncan Bell-Irving, from Vancouver, Canada. One of six brothers to serve in World War 1 (three in the RFC), following service with the army he became an observer prior to pilot training. Shot down in September 1915 he survived unhurt, although he was wounded in December. Becoming a pilot, Bell-Irving joined No 60 Sqn in May 1916, and by mid-October had achieved seven combat victories and been awarded the MC. Six of his claims had been whilst flying Nieuport A203 (his first victory had been in a Morane). He was shot down again on 21 October, and once more emerged unhurt, but finally, on 9 November, whilst flying A272, he was shot down again and was wounded. Bell-Irving received a Bar to his MC and the French *Croix de Guerre*, and after recovery, served with (and later commanded) the School of Special Flying at Gosport till war's end. He died in 1965.

Capt W A Bishop was another Canadian to serve with No 60 Sqn. In 1917 he personally claimed 36 victories, including three on 2 June during a raid, which he described, was upon a German airfield, although no German records substantiate this action. He did however, receive the VC. Flying SE 5s in the summer of 1917, Bishop brought his claims to 47, and whilst commanding No 85 Sqn the following spring, took his total 'claims' to 72 – all 25 in less than a month or, to be precise, 12 actual days!

Referred to earlier, Capt K L Caldwell came from New Zealand. His first victory was scored whilst flying with No 8 Sqn (BE 2d), but he joined No 60 Sqn in late 1916, and by September 1917 had scored seven more victories, six flying B1654. Caldwell had also become a flight commander and won the MC. In 1918 he commanded No 74 Sqn, and by the end of the war had scored 25 victories and received the DFC and Bar and Belgian *Croix de Guerre*. Keith 'Grid' Caldwell served again in World War 2, attaining the rank of air commodore (CBE). A farmer by profession, he died in November 1980.

Capt W M 'Willy' Fry MC was another fighter pilot who went through the two-seater school of action (with No 8 Sqn) prior to being posted

One of the RFC's earliest Nieuport aces was Capt Duncan Bell-Irving of No 60 Sqn who, in 1916, scored seven victories – six of them in Nieuport A203

Maj Keith 'Grid' Caldwell was CO of No 74 Sqn in 1918. The previous year he had flown with No 60 Sqn, where he had achieved seven of his 25 victories flying Nieuports. At least six of these kills had been scored in B1654 (*via Paul Sautehaug*)

onto scouts. He saw action during the Somme battles with No 11 Sqn, and like Ball was still with this unit when it was absorbed into No 60 Sqn. He became an ace with the latter unit, and was then sent to No 23 Sqn as a flight commander, flying SPADs and Dolphins. Fry's 11th, and last victory, was with No 79 Sqn. He became a wing commander postwar, and saw further active service in World War 2. 'Willy' Fry died in August 1992, one of the last 'Knights' of World War 1.

Capt S B 'Nigger' Horn scored two Nieuport victories and became an ace with No 60 Sqn on SE 5s, winning the MC. Later, as a flight commander with No 85 Sqn, he brought his score to 13 by war's end. His brother commanded No 54 Sqn during World War 1.

Lt W E Jenkins was still only 18 on the occasion of his first victory with No 60 Sqn, claimed on 11 May 1917. He became an ace six days after his 19th birthday, on 15 July. One of his 'out of control' claims was over German ace Adolf von Tutschek, who was forced to land on 29 June. Four of Jenkins' victories were in B1629. Flying SE 5s, he had raised his score to ten by November 1917, but was killed then killed in a mid-air collision on the 23rd.

Almost an ace on Nieuports was Capt Henry 'Duke' Meintjes MC, a 24-year old South African from Springfontein. He flew with No 60 Sqn from 1916 through to February 1917, and claimed four kills before becoming a flight commander with No 56 Sqn. He doubled his score with this unit and won the MC, and later, as an instructor, was recipient of an AFC. After the war Meintjes joined the South African Air Force.

Maj W E Molesworth, or 'Moley' as he was called, came from Ireland, and after serving in the army flew with No 60 Sqn from March to August 1917, commanding 'A' Flight from May. He won the MC and gained four victories on Nieuports, then two on SE 5s. As mentioned earlier, Molesworth then went to No 29 Sqn, where he raised his score to 18. All of his remaining kills were scored flying Nieuports.

Lt S L G 'Poppy' Pope was another Irishman, from Dublin. He served with No 60 Sqn during the summer of 1917, gaining two Nieuport victories in June, then a further four on SE 5s. Winning the MC, he was wounded on 18 November. Remaining in the postwar RAF, and with an AFC, he commanded RAF Debden as World War 2 began.

Maj A J L 'Jack' Scott was one of those 'fighting COs', and flew whenever he could. Between March and July 1917 he scored five victories (three flying B1575), including one *Jasta* 3 machine brought down inside British lines (G.43). He was never a good pilot, and unlike German aces who decorated their huts with pieces from their victim's aeroplanes, Scott decorated his own office with bits of his own smashed Nieuports! On one occasion, on 28 May 1917, he was shot down by Karl Allmenrˆder of *Jasta* 11, becoming the German ace's 21st victory, but he survived. Wounded in the arm on 10 July, he later took command of the Central Flying School, receiving the AFC, and was promoted to lieutenant-colonel. Scott wrote the history of No 60 Sqn, and died in 1922 of double pneumonia.

Capt F O 'Mongoose' Soden was another high-scoring ace who began his career on Nieuports. His first two claims were scored on the type before the arrival of the SE 5. With this latter type he brought his score to 27, flying in turn with Nos 60 and 41 Sqns, and won the DFC. He added a Bar to this in 1922 with No 1 Sqn, flying in Iraq. At one time in World War 2 Soden was also commanding officer of RAF Biggin Hill. He died in February 1961.

MARKINGS

As far as is known No 60 Sqn did not use specific markings on its Nieuports, instead adorning individual aircraft with numbers in red behind the fuselage roundel. Later, each flight also carried the flight letter (e.g. 'A-6'), which was applied ahead of the roundel, with the number aft of it. These were red on silver-doped machines and white on camouflaged ones. Like other units, No 60 Sqn also went through a period of using silver-doped machines, and some were later camouflaged – occasionally both at the same time.

NO 111 SQN

Many of the war-weary Nieuport Scouts from the Western Front found their way to the Middle East in the latter half of 1917, several going to No 111 Sqn in Palestine. All had their former unit markings overpainted, and can only be identified by their serial numbers. Aircraft flown by several aces were, of course, among those that wound up in the Middle East, including Ball's, Mannock's and Hilton's.

'Treble One' had been formed from a flight of No 14 Sqn at Deir-el-Ballah, in Palestine, on 1 August 1917, and had received a variety of aircraft types including Bristol F 2b Fighters, SE 5s and Nieuports. It produced no aces on Nieuports, but there were aces who flew the French fighter.

Capt Alan J Bott was one. He had previously been an observer with No 70 Sqn in France, often flying with Capt A M Vaucour. In this capacity, Bott had secured three victories prior to pilot training. In Palestine, he gained two Nieuport victories during April 1918 (in B3595) to become an ace. Bott had won the MC in France and added a Bar in Palestine before being taken prisoner on 22 April. He wrote two books, *An Airman's Outings* and *Eastern Nights – and Flights* under his pen name of 'Contact'. He died in 1952.

Maj R M Drummond MC, an Australian known as 'Peter', gained four victories with No 111 Sqn's Bristol Fighters during December 1917, then four more with Nieuport B3597 – three of them in one action on 27 March 1918. He received the DSO and Bar, and during World War 2 rose to the rank of air marshal and was knighted. Drummond was killed in a flying accident in March 1945.

NO 1 NAVAL WING/NO 1 NAVAL SQUADRON

A number of RNAS pilots flew Nieuports, some of them later becoming aces on other types such as Sopwith Triplanes, Pups or Camels. Like other Naval wings and squadrons, No 1 Naval Wing used a variety of machines including Nieuport Scouts in 1916-17. Flt Sub-Lt S M Kinkead, a South African from Johannesburg, who had joined the RNAS in 1915, saw his first successes flying Nieuports. In August 1916 he had downed two (perhaps three) aircraft, firstly flying a Bristol Scout and then the Nieuport with No 3 Naval Wing.

Maj A J L 'Jack' Scott commanded No 60 Sqn in 1917, during which time he claimed five combat victories. On one occasion he was shot down in Nieuport Scout B1575 by the German ace Karl Allmenröder of the high-scoring *Jasta* 11 (Scott was his 21st kill), although he survived. Scott died of pneumonia in 1922

When No 1 Wing 'A' Squadron became No 1 Naval Squadron, flying Triplanes, Kinkead claimed six victories in October and November 1917. Once the unit re-equipped with Camels, he had brought his tally to 18 by the time the RAF was formed, and he subsequently served as a flight commander with No 201 Sqn until war's end – by which time he had claimed in excess of 30 kills. This famous airmen later flew in North Russia, where he gained further victories over Bolshevik aircraft. Kinkead won the DSO, which he added to his previously earned DSC and Bar and DFC and Bar, making him one of the most highly decorated fighter pilots of the war years. Sadly, he was killed flying the Supermarine S 5 floatplane with the RAF Schneider Trophy Team on 12 March 1928.

An Australian to gain fame in World War 1 had been R S Dallas. He too began scoring with No 1 Naval Wing Nieuport 11s in 1916 with four victories. Flying Triplanes, he then brought his score to 20 by August 1917. Dallas' final score was 32, gained while flying Camels and then as CO of No 40 Sqn, on SE 5s, in 1918. He was killed in action on 1 June 1918, having been awarded the DSO, DSC and Bar.

No 6 Naval Squadron

Formed in December 1916 at Petit Synthe, near Dunkirk, this unit was attached to the RFC in March 1917, at which time it was equipped with Nieuport 17 Scouts. It took part in the severe fighting of that spring, and one of its pilots achieved ace status.

Flt Cdr E W Norton had earlier flown Nieuports with No 1 Naval Wing, and claimed his first victory over Ostend on 20 October 1916, as already mentioned. This was a kite balloon which he destroyed with Le Prieur rockets, for which he received the DSC. With 6 Naval he commanded a flight, and had shot down a further eight German machines by the end of 'Bloody April'. Three of these were in N3187 and three in N3208. Norton was injured in a crash involving the former fighter on 9 April, the machine being burnt out. Later in the war he commanded No 204 Sqn (Camels), and postwar became a group captain.

The only Nieuport ace to serve with No 6 Naval Squadron was E W Norton, who claimed all nine of his victories between October 1916 and the end of April 1917. He scored 'doubles' on 5 and 9 April and a 'triple' on the 29th of that same month. Norton ended the war as a major in the RAF, and eventually rose to the rank of group captain in the 1930s

Australian Lt R S Dallas poses in front of a Type 11. He scored his first three victories (out of an eventual total of 32) flying Nieuport Scouts with No 1 Naval Wing in 1916. The bulk of Dallas' impressive tally came while flying Camels and then as CO of No 40 Sqn, on SE 5s, in 1918. He was killed in action on 1 June 1918 (*Bruce/Leslie collection*)

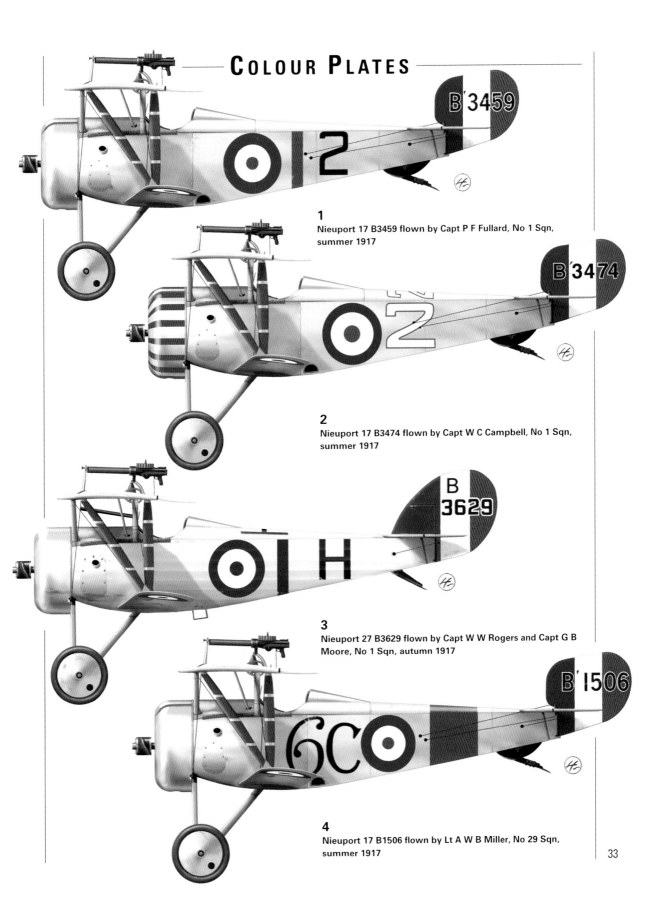

1
Nieuport 17 B3459 flown by Capt P F Fullard, No 1 Sqn,
summer 1917

2
Nieuport 17 B3474 flown by Capt W C Campbell, No 1 Sqn,
summer 1917

3
Nieuport 27 B3629 flown by Capt W W Rogers and Capt G B
Moore, No 1 Sqn, autumn 1917

4
Nieuport 17 B1506 flown by Lt A W B Miller, No 29 Sqn,
summer 1917

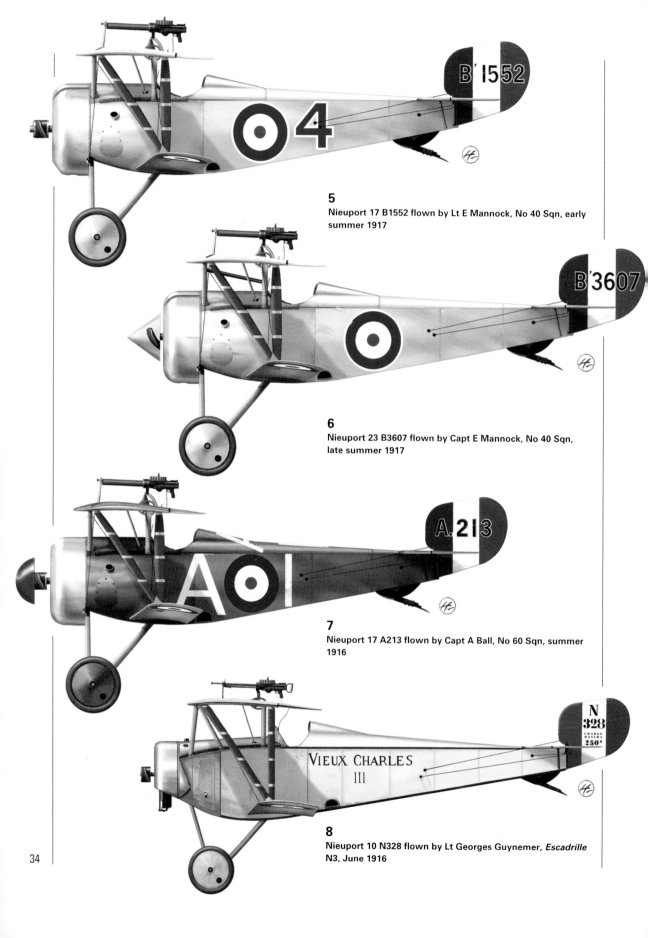

5
Nieuport 17 B1552 flown by Lt E Mannock, No 40 Sqn, early summer 1917

6
Nieuport 23 B3607 flown by Capt E Mannock, No 40 Sqn, late summer 1917

7
Nieuport 17 A213 flown by Capt A Ball, No 60 Sqn, summer 1916

8
Nieuport 10 N328 flown by Lt Georges Guynemer, *Escadrille N3*, June 1916

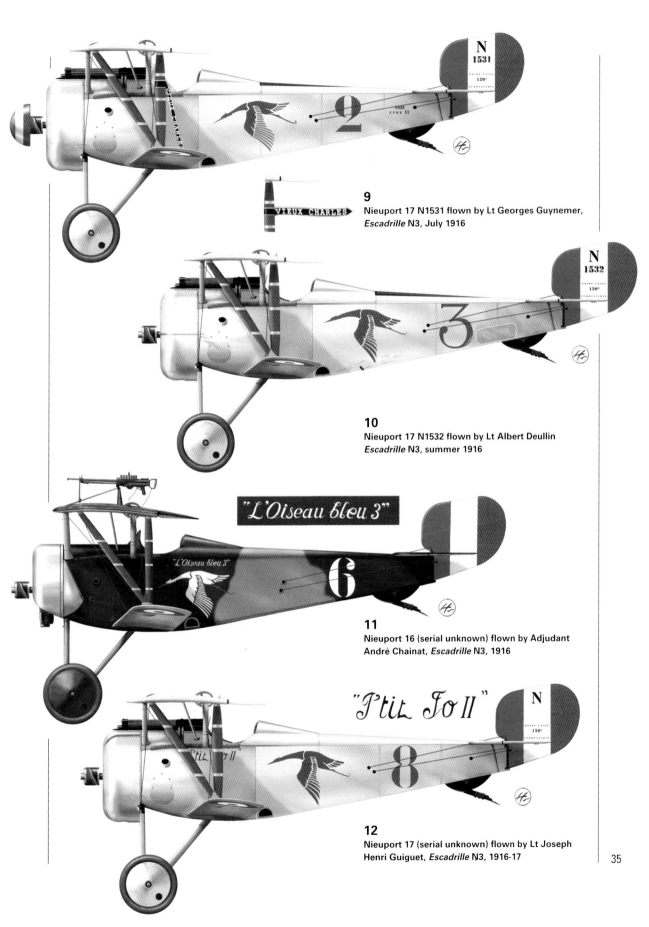

9
Nieuport 17 N1531 flown by Lt Georges Guynemer,
Escadrille N3, July 1916

10
Nieuport 17 N1532 flown by Lt Albert Deullin
Escadrille N3, summer 1916

11
Nieuport 16 (serial unknown) flown by Adjudant
André Chainat, *Escadrille* N3, 1916

12
Nieuport 17 (serial unknown) flown by Lt Joseph
Henri Guiguet, *Escadrille* N3, 1916-17

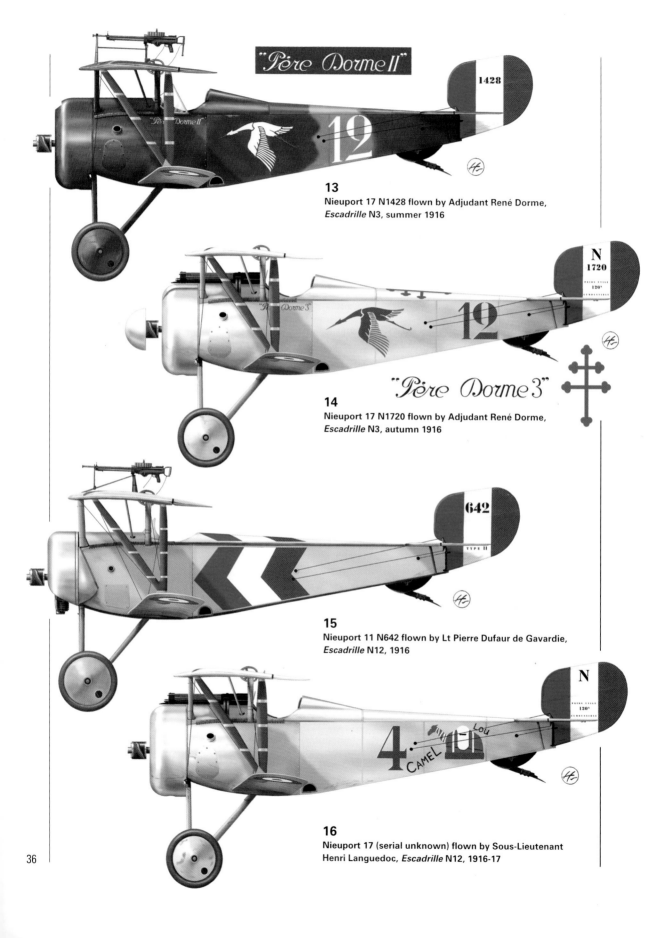

"Père Dorme II"

13
Nieuport 17 N1428 flown by Adjudant René Dorme,
Escadrille N3, summer 1916

"Père Dorme 3"

14
Nieuport 17 N1720 flown by Adjudant René Dorme,
Escadrille N3, autumn 1916

15
Nieuport 11 N642 flown by Lt Pierre Dufaur de Gavardie,
Escadrille N12, 1916

16
Nieuport 17 (serial unknown) flown by Sous-Lieutenant
Henri Languedoc, *Escadrille* N12, 1916-17

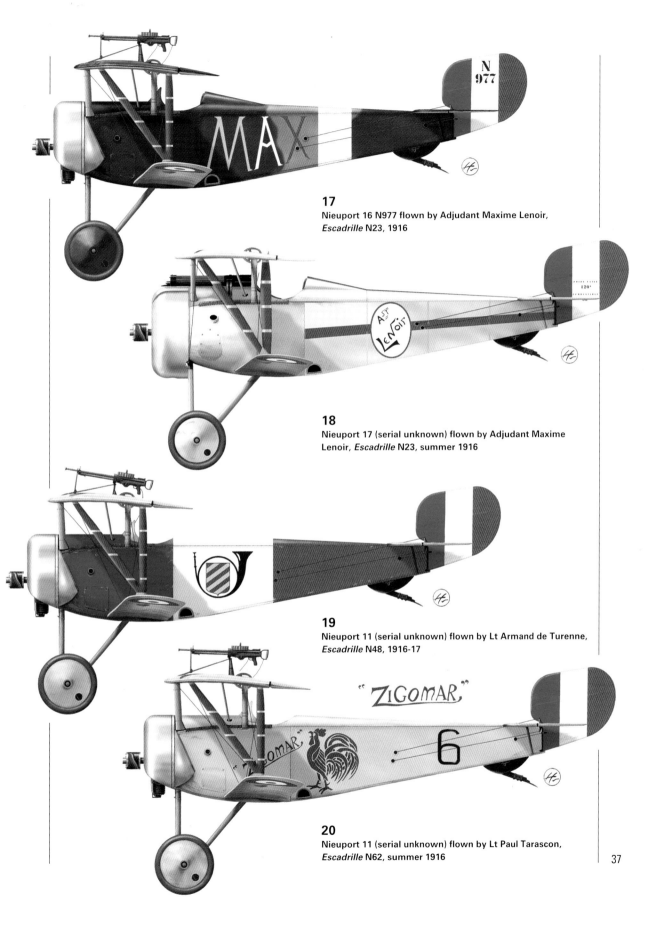

17
Nieuport 16 N977 flown by Adjudant Maxime Lenoir,
Escadrille N23, 1916

18
Nieuport 17 (serial unknown) flown by Adjudant Maxime
Lenoir, *Escadrille* N23, summer 1916

19
Nieuport 11 (serial unknown) flown by Lt Armand de Turenne,
Escadrille N48, 1916-17

20
Nieuport 11 (serial unknown) flown by Lt Paul Tarascon,
Escadrille N62, summer 1916

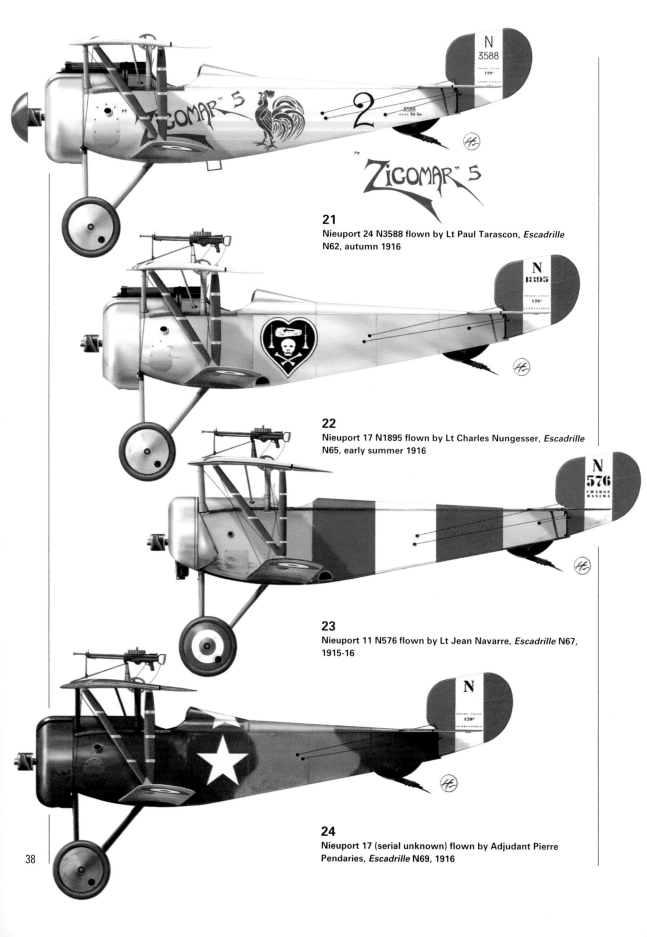

"ZIGOMAR" 5

21
Nieuport 24 N3588 flown by Lt Paul Tarascon, *Escadrille* N62, autumn 1916

22
Nieuport 17 N1895 flown by Lt Charles Nungesser, *Escadrille* N65, early summer 1916

23
Nieuport 11 N576 flown by Lt Jean Navarre, *Escadrille* N67, 1915-16

24
Nieuport 17 (serial unknown) flown by Adjudant Pierre Pendaries, *Escadrille* N69, 1916

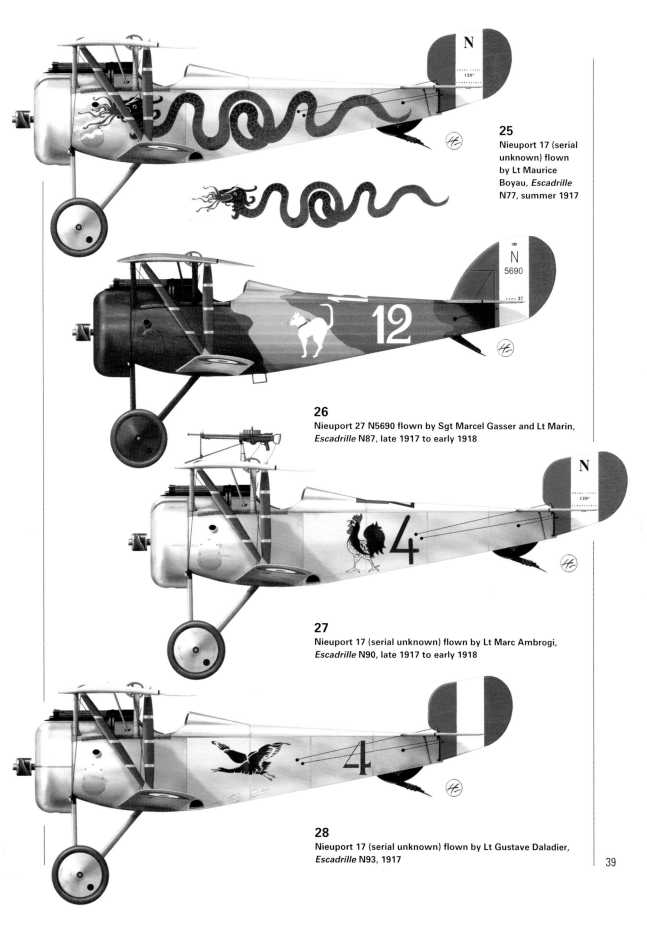

25
Nieuport 17 (serial unknown) flown by Lt Maurice Boyau, *Escadrille* N77, summer 1917

26
Nieuport 27 N5690 flown by Sgt Marcel Gasser and Lt Marin, *Escadrille* N87, late 1917 to early 1918

27
Nieuport 17 (serial unknown) flown by Lt Marc Ambrogi, *Escadrille* N90, late 1917 to early 1918

28
Nieuport 17 (serial unknown) flown by Lt Gustave Daladier, *Escadrille* N93, 1917

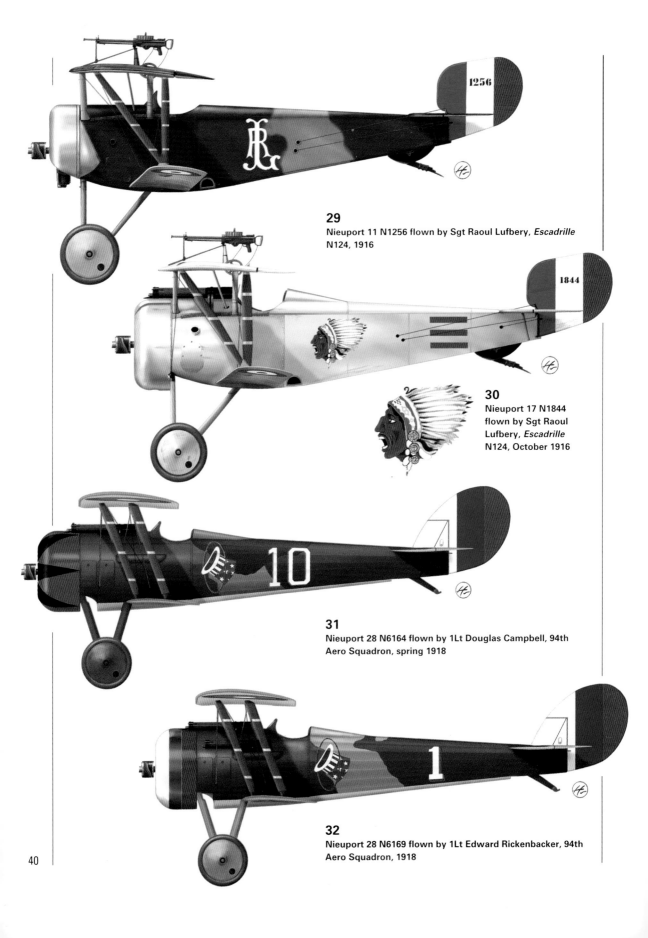

29
Nieuport 11 N1256 flown by Sgt Raoul Lufbery, *Escadrille* N124, 1916

30
Nieuport 17 N1844 flown by Sgt Raoul Lufbery, *Escadrille* N124, October 1916

31
Nieuport 28 N6164 flown by 1Lt Douglas Campbell, 94th Aero Squadron, spring 1918

32
Nieuport 28 N6169 flown by 1Lt Edward Rickenbacker, 94th Aero Squadron, 1918

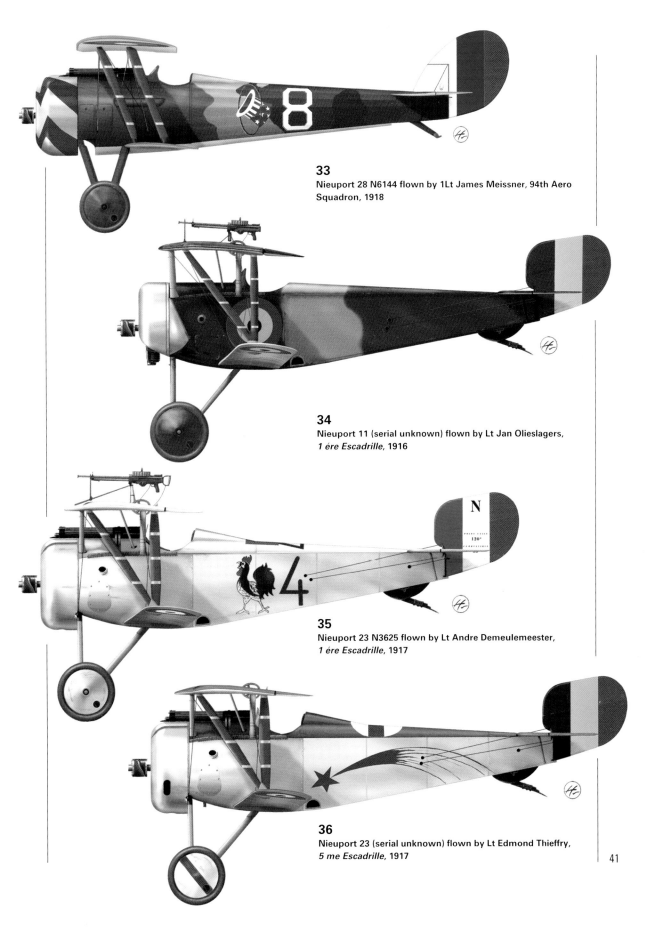

33
Nieuport 28 N6144 flown by 1Lt James Meissner, 94th Aero
Squadron, 1918

34
Nieuport 11 (serial unknown) flown by Lt Jan Olieslagers,
1 ére Escadrille, 1916

35
Nieuport 23 N3625 flown by Lt Andre Demeulemeester,
1 ére Escadrille, 1917

36
Nieuport 23 (serial unknown) flown by Lt Edmond Thieffry,
5 me Escadrille, 1917

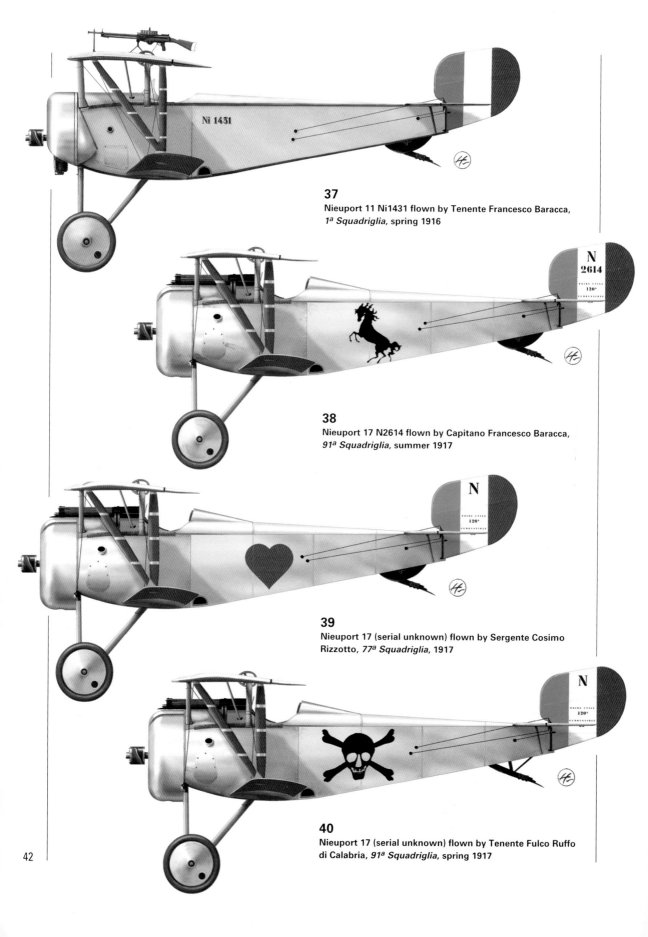

37
Nieuport 11 Ni1431 flown by Tenente Francesco Baracca,
1ª Squadriglia, spring 1916

38
Nieuport 17 N2614 flown by Capitano Francesco Baracca,
91ª Squadriglia, summer 1917

39
Nieuport 17 (serial unknown) flown by Sergente Cosimo
Rizzotto, *77ª Squadriglia*, 1917

40
Nieuport 17 (serial unknown) flown by Tenente Fulco Ruffo
di Calabria, *91ª Squadriglia*, spring 1917

FRENCH ACES

Naturally, the French used the nimble Nieuport sesquiplane in numbers prior to the arrival of the more robust SPAD VII, with many aces being produced on the type. Still others began their successful frontline careers on the Nieuport, before moving on to SPADs.

It is not always possible to be certain which victories were scored on which type. One would have thought the *escadrille* designation would help here, with the prefix 'N' standing for Nieuport and 'SPA' for SPAD. However, an *escadrille* could operate both types, and even when fully re-equipped with SPADs, it took a while for headquarters to confirm in orders the change of designation from 'N' to 'SPA'.

One of the most famous *escadrilles* was N3. From humble beginnings it had become part of the *Groupe de Cachy* at the time of the Verdun battle. Commanded by Felix Brocard, it boasted a number of France's premier air fighters. Unlike the British, the French (like the Germans) lauded their successful fighter pilots, and all became well known to the French people. Newspapers and magazines lionised their prowess in combat, and these much-bemedaled heroes of France became familiar to everyone through postcard pictures featuring their faces.

The most well-known of N3's

The exceptional Georges Guynemer of N3 flew a variety of Nieuports during his long career at the Front, most of which bore his personal insignia, *LE VIEUX CHARLES*. This Nieuport 11 (N836) was used by him at Verdun in the early spring of 1916

successful pilots was the amazing Georges Guynemer. A man of frail stature and initially frail health, he nevertheless was a marvel in the air, and soon became the darling of French aviation and an adoring public. With the French army bleeding to death at Verdun during 1916-17, it was not difficult to see how airmen fighting above the carnage of wire, trenches, machine-gun and shell fire could be seen as chivalrous 'knights of the air'.

Georges Marie Ludovic Jules Guynemer came from Paris, and in November 1914 volunteered to serve his country just a month before his 20th birthday. Not being a robust person, he chose to be a mechanic in the air service, but soon decided to train as a pilot, which he had achieved by April 1915. He was sent to MS3 (*escadrille* 3, flying Morane-Saulnier machines, which as the equipment moved to Nieuports became N3) as a corporal, before being promoted to sergeant. Guynemer's first success came in a Morane, but then the Nieuports arrived and by the end of the year he had four victories, the *Médaille Militaire*, and had been made a *Chevalier de la Légion d'Honneur*. He had also become a commissioned officer.

A close-up of Guynemer's personal insignia worn on Nieuport 10 N328, which shows the *III* below the name, rather than after the word *CHARLES*, as has sometimes appeared in published artwork of this aircraft

Guynemer with yet another style of his personal insignia. Successful aces often flew many different machines during their time in combat

Guynemer and Cdt Felix Brocard (to the ace's left) are seen in conversation alongside the former's Nieuport 17 N1531 'red 2'. The aircraft also wears the red stork emblem of N3 on its silver-doped fuselage. Note the *cône de penetration* fitted forward of the propeller, this device being used for a brief period in order to try and overcome the drag associated with the fighter's blunt rotary engine and cowling

Escadrille N3 carried a *cigogne* (stork) emblem on its aircraft, and as soon as the *Groupe de Cachy*, to which it belonged, became *Groupe de Combat 12*, with its three other units also carrying variations of a stork emblem, it became known as *les Cigognes*, and was soon associated with the élite of the French fighter pilots. This was not wholly true, but GC12 and N3 in particular did have a number of highly successful fighter aces within its ranks. During 1916 Guynemer brought his score to 25 confirmed victories, more than half on Nieuports. Unlike the British, French pilots were only given credit for aircraft witnessed by others as destroyed, their 'probables' only being noted, but not counted, in a pilot's score.

Capitaine Guynemer went on to achieve 53 victories, with another 35 probables. He became an Officer of the *Légion d'Honneur* and his *Croix de Guerre* ribbon was adorned by over 20 *Palmes*, each representing a citation in orders. In addition, he received the British DSO and the Belgian Order of Leopold. He was killed in action on 11 September 1917.

Rene Pierre Marie Dorme was also 20 years old as the war began, yet despite this he was known as *Pére* ('father' or perhaps 'papa'). He had served as an artillery man in North Africa before becoming a pilot. Injured in a crash, Dorme did not see action until March 1916, but in June he was sent to join N3. It was

'Pére' Dorme of N 3 was the victor in over 23 combats with the enemy, at least half of these seeing him at the controls of a Nieuport Scout. He was killed in action on 25 May 1917 whilst flying a SPAD VII in a fight with Heinrich Kroll of *Jasta* 9. Dorme was the German's fifth victory

Dorme's Nieuport 17 (N1428) wore his personal number '12' on its camouflaged fuselage sides. Later, this marking was also applied to the top starboard wing

Three Nieuport aces, namely (from left to right) Alfred Hertaux of N3 and Georges Flachaire and Marcel Viallet from N67. Note the variety of uniforms, which was a feature of all flying services in World War 1

still the period of the 'lone wolf' air fighter, and Dorme, like Ball in the RFC, liked to hunt and fight alone, seeking out German observation aircraft, but he was also a good man in a patrol. By the end of 1916 he had 17 kills, and his score had risen to 23 by May 1917. What is more he is reputed to have scored some 70 probables. While this seems excessive, their are notations referring to at least 17. Having been awarded the *Légion d'Honneur*, *Medaille Militaire* and *Croix de Guerre*, Dorme was killed in action on 25 May 1917, shot down by Heinrich Kroll of *Jasta* 9.

Capitaine Alfred Marie Joseph Heurtaux came from Nantes, and like so many officers had passed through the St Cyr Military College. Serving with the Hussars, he had been commissioned in August 1914 at the age of 21. In the early part of the war he was cited four times for bravery prior to transferring to the air service, first as an observer, then taking pilot training. Following time with MS38, Heurtaux was assigned to N3 in June 1916. After his fourth victory on 3 August he became a *Chevalier de la Légion d'Honneur.* He now also commanded the *escadrille.*

Heurtaux became an ace on Nieuports before he was seriously wounded on 5 May 1917, by which time N3 had moved on to SPAD fighters. In all he claimed 21 victories and 13 probables. Although he returned to his command in August, Heurtaux was wounded again in September, which put him out of action for the rest of the war. He became an Officer of the *Légion d'Honneur* and received the *Croix de Guerre* with 15 *Palmes* and two *Etoiles de Bronze*. In World War 2 he was the Inspector of Fighter Avi-

André Chainat scored ten victories with N3 before a bad wound on 7 September 1916 put him out of the active war for good

This Type 17 was flown by N3 ace Albert Deullin, who claimed 11 of his 20 kills in Nieuports. The two pilots are Deullin (left) and Paul Tarascon, the latter 'making ace' with N62 after leaving N3

ation until the fall of France, when he served with the Resistance until deported to Germany in April 1945. Gen Heurtaux, President of the France Fighter Aces Association, died in Paris.

Andre Julien Chainat scored his ten Nieuport victories between March and August 1916. A former artillery man, he joined N3 in January 1916. Recipient of the *Légion d'Honneur*, *Médaille Militaire*, *Croix de Guerre* with nine *Palmes* and one *Etoile de Bronze*, he was wounded on 16 June and again on 7 September, the latter putting him out of the active war. Chainat died in Cannes on 6 November 1961.

Capitaine Albert Louis Deullin was another who scored well on Nieuports, 11 of his 20 victories being claimed on the type. Slightly older than others in the *Escadrille*, the former dragoon was 27 at the height of his fame. He had already seen action with MF62 prior to his posting to N3, and been decorated. After his 11th victory with the latter unit, he was given command of SPA73 in February 1917, and later led *Groupe de Combat* 19 in 1918. With N3 Deullin was made a *Chevalier de la Légion d'Honneur* (and an Officer of the order as commander of GC19), and also received the *Croix de Guerre* with 14 *Palmes*. He was killed in a flying accident on 29 May 1923 at Villacoublay.

Another *Cigogne* ace was Capitaine Mathieu Marie Joseph Antoine Tenant de la Tour, yet another Paris-born former cavalry officer. Transferring to aviation, he became a pilot in May 1915 but was injured in an accident in October. His first posting was to N57 in December, where he gained his first victory on 25 January 1916 – a shared balloon kill. It was a dismal day with fog, de la Tour suddenly coming upon the balloon as it emerged 'through a sea of fog'. One of the observers had a machine-gun, but the Frenchman knocked him

Mathieu Tenant de la Tour, Alfred Hertaux, Albert Deullin and Georges Guynemer all achieved 'acedom' with N3. Again, note the variety of uniforms and the *Cigogne* badge on Guynemer's tunic

out then attacked again as the balloon was pulled down. He and his leader finally set it afire just 50 metres from the ground. Although he was lost in the mist, he managed to find his way back across the lines to safety. He was made a *Chevalier de la Légion d'Honneur*.

Wounded in combat on 25 April, de la Tour returned to the front after his injury had healed and was sent to N3. His next victory came on 9 July, but although this was cited, for some reason it was never officially added to his score. His second confirmed kill came on 15 July, and by the end of the year he had raised his score to eight and two probables. The following April he was given command of N26, scoring his ninth, and final, victory on 7 May.

Alfred Victor Robert Auger had been an infantry officer, wounded and decorated before becoming a pilot. Flying with C11, he was wounded again on 8 July 1915, but then requested an assignment as a Nieuport pilot, being sent to N31. In early 1916 Auger scored his first two victories, but was badly injured in a crash on 16 April. Returning to active duty, he went to N3, and although slightly wounded in a fight with four German

Capitaine Alfred Auger flew Nieuports marked '7' with N3, although this machine only seems to feature this number on the top wing and not the fuselage. The photograph was taken at Villers Bretonneux in October 1916

aircraft on the afternoon of 16 February, he was fit enough to take command of the *escadrille* on 17 March. Auger was killed in action on 28 July flying a SPAD, having achieved seven victories. On the fateful day, he battled with five German aircraft but was hit in the neck. Bleeding heavily, he managed to get down behind the lines but died within minutes of coming to a stop. Auger had probably fought with *Jasta* 8 that morning, Vfw Rudolf Franke having lodged an unconfirmed claim. This unit also lost its *Staffelführer* in this fight, so perhaps Auger scored another kill before he was hit.

Escadrille N3 had adopted the stork insignia at an early stage, and it soon became very familiar. Each *escadrille* in the *Groupe* had different stork insignia, but N3's was the most famous. On silver machines it was generally painted in red, while on the camouflaged scouts it was basically white. Individual machines carried numbers on the fuselage sides, repeated on the top starboard wing.

Escadrille N12 fought during the Verdun and Somme battles. Capitaine Joseph Marie Xavier De Sevin had been in the infantry, and had risen through the ranks to sous-lieutenant by mid-1915. He was assigned to N12 in November 1915, flying Nieuport two-seaters and scouts, but it was not until July 1916 that De Sevin scored his first victory. A further eight months would then pass before his second kill was confirmed. By

Capitaine Alfred Auger scored two kills with N31 and five with N3 prior to his death in action on 28 July 1917 flying a SPAD. Note the N3 *Cigogne* badge on his tunic and his 31st Infantry Regiment hat

Joseph-Henri Guigot became an ace whilst serving with three different units. His first claim was made with N95, and this was followed by three more kills with N3 during the winter of 1916-1917. Guigot then had to wait until 24 October 1918 before securing his fifth victory – and ace status – whilst flying with SPA167

Another ace of the 1916 period was Adjudant P H E Dufaur de Gavardie, who scored six victories with N12 before being seriously wounded in February 1917. His Nieuport 11 (N642) carried broad chevrons of red, white and blue on its fuselage

Henri Languedoc of N12 flew this unusually-marked Nieuport 17 in 1917. The origin of these markings is unknown to this author, and they may be some kind of 'play' on his former cavalry career. Having gained seven kills, Languedoc was severely wounded on 16 July 1917 and died two days later

the summer he had achieved six victories, and in December he was given command of SPA26, doubling his score by war's end. De Sevin received the *Légion d'Honneur* and the *Croix de Guerre* with nine *Palmes*. He rose to the rank of major-general in World War 2, and became a Grand Officer of the *Légion d'Honneur*, as well as being made a CBE by the British. De Sevin died on 7 November 1963.

Sous-Lieutenant Henri Francois Languedoc was 31 years old when he gained his first victory on 23 October 1916 flying with N12. Another former cavalry man, he also fought with the infantry but was wounded in 1915 and, unable to serve at the front, transferred to flying. Assigned to fly Nieuports with N12, he had scored seven victories by mid-April 1917, but was badly wounded on 16 July and died two days later. Languedoc was made *Chevalier de la Légion d'Honneur*, and had also been decorated whilst still an infantryman. N12's insignia was that of a white and light

Yet another early Nieuport ace was Adjudant Maxime Lenoir of N23, who claimed nine of his eleven victories whilst flying Nieuports. He was killed in combat on 25 October 1916

blue triangular pennant (*fanion*) with a small black '12' in the centre.

Sous-Lieutenant Lucien Joseph Jailler flew with N15, and having learnt to fly in 1911, he had experienced service with the French air force before the war. Despite this, he started the conflict as a tractor driver, and did not get a flying post until April 1915. Serving with MS15, Jailler was badly wounded in combat on 16 May, but received the *Médaille Militaire*. Recovering, he returned to his unit, which was now flying Nieuports as N12. He scored four victories between March and June 1916 and was then promoted to adjutant in July. He became an ace on 25 September, and by early June 1917 had achieved 12 victories and been made a *Chevalier de la Légion d'Honneur*. Commissioned, Jailler was rested in November and became an instructor. He died due to illness on 2 June 1921, aged 31. N15's insignia was a knight's visored helmet with a white plume flowing back.

Sous-Lieutenant Jean Pie Hyacinthe Paul Jerome Casale, Marquis de Montferato, was born in Corsica and entered military service in 1913 aged 20. At the outbreak of war he requested a transfer to aviation, and by early 1915 was a pilot flying with MF8. He was then assigned to N23, where he scored one victory, before transferring to N76 and then back to N23 on 1 March 1916. Casale became an ace on 10 December 1916, and by the summer of 1917 had gained nine victories, mostly on Nieuports. Awarded the *Médaille Militaire* and *Légion d'Honneur*, he was commissioned and transferred to SPA156, then to SPA38. With the latter unit he had brought his score to 13 by November 1918. Casale was killed in an air crash on 23 June 1923 flying a Bleriot 115 quadrimotor.

Escadrille N23 became such when it exchanged its Moranes for Nieuports in September 1916. The *escadrille* carried a triangular pennant on the fuselage in white with a bright red horizontal-striped centre.

Adjudant Maxime Albert Lenoir had become a pilot in 1913, so was mobilised when the war started. As soon as his military training was completed, he went to C18 and achieved two victories in June 1915. Sent to train on single-seaters, Lenoir was posted to N23 in early 1916, and scored his first Nieuport kill on 17 March. Victory number four came three months later, and by September he had 11 victories, the *Médaille Militaire* and had been made a *Chevalier de la Légion d'Honneur*. Wounded on 9 August and again on 25 September, Lenoir continued flying, only to fall in combat on 25 October 1916. He was 27.

Escadrille N26 produced two Nieuport aces. The first was Sous-Lieutenant Noel Hugues Anne Louis De Rochefort. His military career did not get off to a good start, for whilst serving as a driver he became ill, and for some months was in hospital. Once well again, he volunteered for aviation, and in October 1915 went to N26. After his first victory on 12 March 1916, De Rochefort received the *Médaille Militaire* and, in June, he was made a *Chevalier de la Légion d'Honneur*. By September he had scored seven victories and five probables. He was commissioned, but the 28-year-old ace was shot down flying Nieuport 17bis N1581 on 15 September. De Rochefort died of his wounds the next day.

Constant Frederic Soulier, born in Paris in September 1897, was ten years younger than De Rochfort. He joined the artillery in March 1915, but then learnt to fly. Posted to N26, he gained his first victory on 24 August 1916 – a balloon – and had scored two kills by the time he went into hospital in January 1917. Returning to the *escadrille* in March, Soulier became an ace on 27 May, taking Sauvage's place as the youngest Frenchman to achieve this feat due to the death of his 19-year-old contemporary. Soulier had to return to hospital at the end of June, and was not discharged until the beginning of December. His combat days were over, and he was sent to America to demonstrate combat flying to the US Air Service pilots. In addition to his six kills, Soulier had nine probables and damaged, for which he received the *Médaille Militaire* and the *Croix de Guerre* with six *Palmes* and one *Etoile de Vermeil*. He died in July 1933.

Part of the Storks *groupe*, the insignia of N26 consisted of an elongated version of the bird, usually in black and white with red beak and legs.

Capitaine Georges Felix Madon was the star of N38. Born in Tunisia in July 1892, he learnt to fly in 1911. Joining the army pre-war, he was in aviation by the time war came, flying Bleriot machines. Later, whilst at the controls of a Farman, Madon and his observer came down in Switzerland and were interned. He managed to escape in late 1915. By 1916 he was a fighter pilot, and in early 1917 became an ace. By the time N38 became SPA38, Madon had achieved 25 victories, although some of these would have been scored with the SPAD. By the beginning of September 1918 he had claimed 41 victories. Madon was killed in a flying accident in Tunis on 11 November 1924 – the sixth anniversary of the Armistice.

Top-scoring pilot in *Escadrille* N38 was Georges Felix Madon, who ended the war with 41 kills. More than a dozen of these victories were scored while the unit was equipped with Nieuport Scouts. Madon was killed in a flying accident on 11 November 1924 – the anniversary of the Armistice

Capitaine Armand Jean Galliot Joseph, Marquis de Turenne, came from Le Mans, born in April 1891. A pre-war cavalryman, he transferred to aviation after the war had started. Eventually, he was assigned to N48 in June 1916 and gained his first success in November. By the summer of 1917 Joseph was an ace. With six victories, he went to SPA12 as its commander, and ended the war with 15 kills. He died in December 1980.

There were three Nieuport aces within N57. Parisian Jean Chaput was yet another pre-war infantryman who transferred to aviation as the war started. His first assignment was to MF28, where he rose through the NCO ranks. Wounded on two occasions, Chaput received the *Médaille Militaire* with C28 after scoring a victory on 12 June (the unit having changed from Maurice Farmans to Caudrons), and in March 1916 he was

Nieuport 17 N2186 was flown by N48's Lt Armand de Turenne in 1917. The ace scored six of his fifteen victories while on Nieuports

Armand de Turenne poses alongside an Albatros D V that he and Capitaine J G F Matton shot down on 6 July 1917. The German aircraft, flown by Vfw Manfred Stimmel of *Jasta* 32, crashed at 11.50 am between Courcy and Thil, near Reims. Its pilot was taken prisoner

commissioned. Assigned to N57 in May, he had scored an additional seven kills by the time he was wounded on 24 August and was made a *Chevalier de la Légion d'Honneur*. Chaput returned to N57, but by then it was about to become SPA57 as SPADs arrived.

By April 1918 Chaput's score had risen to 16, one of these victories being the shared claim over Ltn Erich Thomas, a ten-kill ace with *Jasta* 22, on 23 March 1918. He added the British Military Cross to his awards in April, but fell in action just weeks later on 6 May 1918, shot down by Hermann Becker of *Jasta* 12 – the German's tenth of 23 victories. Chaput was 24 years old.

Adjudant Chef Victor Louis Georges Sayaret transferred from the dragoons to the air service soon after war was declared and flew Voisins with V24. On 18 June 1915 he was credited with his first victory, and in May 1916 he transferred to N57 to fly fighters. By the end of the year Sayaret had achieved a total of six victories, won the *Medaille Militaire* and become a *Chevalier de la Légion d'Honneur*. He was then posted to N76 where, on 5 June 1917, he downed his seventh victory, with three more probables noted – Sayaret's third success, scored on 4 August 1917, had been shared with Raoul Lufbery of N124 (his third too). After the war, Sayaret flew with the Mail Service and later as a test pilot with Farmans between 1924-27. Later still, he was a civil pilot with CIDNA and then Air France, flying to Dakar.

The third ace in *Escadrille* N57 was Adjudant Pierre Augustin Francois Violet-Marty. From the Pyranees region, he joined the artillery when war came, but soon decided to fly. In May 1915 he went to MF55, where he won the *Médaille Militaire* on 17 September 1916, then requested a transfer to fighters. Assigned to N57 on 29 September, Violet-Marty had scored five victories by the end of 1916, and added a British Military Medal to his collection, which hung next to his *Croix de Guerre* with five

Despite having lost a foot in a flying accident pre-war, Paul Tarascon (right) achieved 'acedom' with N62 in 1916. This Nieuport 11, marked with a black '6' and his personal black and red rooster emblem, also bore the name *"ZIGOMAR"* (possibly in red) beneath the cockpit. Tarascon's rooster was later adopted as the *escadrille* insignia of N62

Palmes and one *Etoile de Vermeil*. He was killed in action on 27 December in a fight which secured for him his fourth and fifth victories, but at the cost of his own life. Violet-Marty was also credited with three probable victories.

Aircraft from N57 wore a white seabird as their unit insignia, its outstretched wings in an attitude suggesting that the bird was flying away to the left.

Escadrille N62 also produced two Nieuport aces. First was Marcel Robert Leopold Bloch who was from Switzerland, and was 24 when war began. His first posting was to N3, but he then moved to N62 on 25 May 1916. Between 26 June and 1 October Bloch burned five German kite balloons to become an ace, and received the *Médaille Militaire*. In 1917 he went with the Military Mission to Russia, but he saw no further frontline service. He received the *Légion d'Honneur* and Russian decorations. Bloch died in March 1938.

The other ace with N62 was Paul Albert Pierre Tarascon. In 1901, when he was 19, he entered the military and served with the Colonial Infantry. Interested in aviation, he began learning to fly in 1911 but suffered a bad crash and had to have his right foot amputated. This did not deter him, and when war came Tarascon volunteered to fly, and in January 1915 he completed his training and became an instructor. He saw active duty with N31 and then N3, but by the late spring of 1916 was sent to N62, where he began his successful career. By the autumn Tarascon had shot down eight German aircraft, and received the *Médaille Militaire* and *Légion d'Honneur*. Following his unit's re-equipment with SPADs, he raised his score to 12 by mid-1918. Known as the 'ace with the wooden leg', Tarascon survived the war and later became a colonel. In World War 2 he worked with the Resistance, and in 1955 received the Grand Cross to the *Légion d'Honneur*. Tarascon died on 11 June 1977 aged 94.

The *escadrille's* insignia was a black fighting cock with a red comb and orange beak and feet, although a white version was used on camouflaged machines. It was based on a personal insignia first used by Tarascon.

Tarascon's Nieuport 24bis N3588 (fitted with a *cône de penetration*) is shown with the *"ZIGOMAR"* titling now followed by the number *5*. Therefore, it must be assumed that this aircraft was the fifth Nieuport to carry this name

The third-ranking French fighter ace was the incomparable Charles Nungesser of N65. Famed for his injuries, as well as his overall score of 43 victories (almost 30 of which were scored on Nieuports), it was said that he had broken every major bone in his body at least once! He was also well known for his macabre personal insignia – a white-edged black heart, on to which had been painted a coffin, two candle-sticks and a skull and crossbones. Nungesser even went as far as to have a similar badge sewn to his shirt pocket. After having been mistakenly attacked by a British fighter (and forced to shoot it down), he carried broad red, white and blue bands across the upper wing and top fuselage decking of his aircraft in an effort to aid recognition. Nungesser's scouts also occasionally had these bands painted on the upper surfaces of the lower wings as well
(*via Jon Guttman*)

Nungesser's Nieuport 17 N1490, which he flew while attached to N124 *Lafayette* in July 1916. It is painted in green and brown camouflage finish, with a grey cowling and undersides. Finally, the scout boasts both Vickers and Lewis guns

Escadrille N65 had amongst its ranks one of the most heroic of all fighter pilots, proving that the *Cigognes* did not have all the élite French aviators in World War 1. Charles Eugene Jules Marie Nungesser came from Paris, and had worked in South America as a car mechanic pre-war, before becoming a racing driver. A friend of his in South America owned an early Bleriot aeroplane, and Nungesser persuaded the man to let him fly it, which he did with limited instruction! He entered military service as the war began. As a private soldier in the hussars, he saw action as an NCO and won the *Médaille Militaire*.

Requesting a move to aviation, Nungesser became a pilot in early 1915 and was sent to VB106, then moved to N65, having achieved one victory in his Voisin two-seater. However, soon after arriving at his new unit he had taken off without permission, so although he received the *Croix de Guerre*, he was also placed under close arrest for eight days.

**Nungesser's Nieuport 17 N1895.
Note the broad bands across the top
surfaces of both wings**

**Nungesser's Nieuport 25 N5324.
Note that this aircraft has had
roundels painted on the undersides
of its upper wing**

Gaining his second victory in December, Nungesser became a *Chevalier de la Légion d'Honneur*. Badly injured in a crash on 6 February 1916 which saw both of his legs broken, he returned to be commissioned, and in April began scoring victories. Wounded in combat on 19 May, he was back in action within a few days. By the end of 1916 Nungesser had scored 21 victories, but had been injured again in June. He had also received the Military Cross from the British. In early 1917 Nungesser had to return to hospital because of his earlier injuries, but he managed to persuade his superiors not to ground him. Getting himself attached to V116, with his own Nieuport, he added nine more confirmed kills to his tally by August 1917.

In December Nungesser was injured yet again, this time in a car crash, but after treatment, and a month as an instructor, the ace returned to his old unit – now SPA65. Although the rest of the *escadrille* now flew SPADs, he still continued with later versions of the Nieuport adorned with his distinctive fuselage insignia of a black heart, as well as large red, white and blue stripes on the wings and top decking. In May 1918, with his score at 35, Nungesser was made an Officer of the *Légion d'Honneur*.

A much bemedalled Charles Nungesser is seen wearing both French and foreign decorations, including the British Military Cross (*via Jon Guttman*)

By mid-August (by this time he had switched to a SPAD) Nungesser had scored a total of 43 victories, plus 11 probables. In addition to his other awards he had received the *Croix de Guerre* with 28 *Palmes* and two *Etoiles*, the Belgian *Croix de Guerre* and *Croix de la Couronne de Léopold*, the Montenegro Order of Danilo, the American DSC, the Portuguese *Croix de Guerre*, Russian Cross of Karageorgevitch and the Serbian Cross of Bravery.

Postwar, Nungesser flew many crowd-pulling aerial shows, and then came the chance to fly the Atlantic with an old friend, Francois Coli. The pair took off on 8 May 1927 but were never seen again. It was a sad end to another hero of France, one who had sacrificed much in the Great War. At one stage it was said he had had every major bone in his body broken – at least once, and he often flew before previous injuries had properly healed.

Nungesser had also served with the American volunteers in the *Escadrille Lafayette* between July and August 1916, having become bored

Of all the early French aces, *Escadrille* N67's mercurial Jean Navarre was almost certainly the most famous. Flying this distinctly-marked red, white and blue fuselaged Nieuport 11 (N576), and later an all-red Nieuport 11, his flights over the battlefront at Verdun made him well known to French troops below

Navarre, possibly in his red Nieuport 11. Note the fixed Lewis gun on the top decking (*Bruce/Leslie collection*)

with his convalescence – he had shot down his 11th victory, on 21 July, whilst serving with them The Americans were impressed by this French ace, with his good looks having in no way been diminished by his rows of gold teeth, his natural teeth having been smashed in crashes.

Another N65 ace was Joseph Denis Bernard Robert De Bonnefoy, who had also been a pre-war cavalryman. Soon after war was declared, he volunteered for aviation training and, like Nungesser, first flew Voisins with VB101. After a period as an instructor, he returned to action with N68, followed by N65. With the latter De Bonnefoy downed five aircraft by the end of 1916, then, after transferring to N84 in 1917, gained his seventh, and final, victory on 21 August. After a rest he went to SPA15 and later to BR31. De Bonnefoy ended the war with SPA23. He had received the *Médaille Militaire*, *Légion d'Honneur* and French and Belgian *Croix de Guerres*, and remained in the service postwar. He was later made an Officer of the *Légion d'Honneur* and died on 27 September 1946.

Sergent Paul Joannes Sauvage became a military pilot at 19, and flying with N65 gained his first victory on 9 July 1916, and on 2 October became the youngest ace in the French Air Service, still only 19. In November he received the *Médaille Militaire*. Flying SPADs, Sauvage gained one further victory with N65, then flew with N38, bringing his score to eight and six probables. Back with N65, his SPAD was hit by an anti-aircraft shell on 7 January 1917 and he fell to his death. Sauvage was still a month away from his 20th birthday.

N65 adorned its aircraft with a black dragon, which had black wings and a curling black tongue, much like a Welsh dragon.

Capitaine Jean Marie Emile Derode became an ace with two units. A former dragoon, he transferred to aviation in 1915 and was assigned to N67, where he shot down two German aircraft at the end of the year. Sent to command N102, Derode had brought his score to six and four probables by the early summer. In 1918 he took command of SPA99, where he scored his seventh victory on 4 June, but was then killed in action just moments later. As well as the *Légion d'Honneur*, Derode had received the French and Belgian *Croix de Guerre*.

Just 21 when he joined the artillery in 1914, Sous-Lieutenant Georges Charles Marie Francois Flachaire soon volunteered to fly.

Jean Navarre scored a total of twelve victories, nine of these whilst flying Nieuport Scouts

Sent to N67 on 1 September 1915, he flew two-seaters until single-seaters arrived, then claimed his first victory on 30 April 1916, for which he received the *Médaille Militaire*. This combat had lasted for a prolonged period and, apparently, after Flachaire had ran out of ammunition, he so harassed the German two-seater that its crew was forced to land inside French territory, where they were taken prisoner. By November he had achieved seven victories, and in early 1917 was given the British Military Cross. Flachaire gained one further kill in August 1917, and was then commissioned. Recalled to duty in 1939, he served until the end of that war too, retiring to Venezuela, where he died in April 1973, aged 80.

Probably the most famous of the early aces was Jean Marie Dominique Navarre, a man who claimed he had learnt to fly in 1911 (which, apparently, was untrue), so was immediately accepted into French aviation when war came. He flew with MS8 and MS12, gaining three victories with the latter in 1915, so his aggressiveness led to a fighter assignment – N67. By this time he had already received the *Médaille Militaire* and the *Légion d'Honneur*. Navarre's first claims in N67 came on 26 February 1916, when he achieved one of the first 'double' scores of the war, which also made him an ace. By the time he had scored his eighth victory Navarre had been commissioned, and by 17 June, when he was wounded, he had a total of 12 victories, with 15 probables.

In the latter half of the war Navarre spent much of his time in medical care following the onset of mental health problems, the ace having 'burned himself out' in the air, especially above Verdun. He had flown constantly over the embattled town, where his red Nieuport became a familiar sight to the ground troops of both sides. After the war Navarre became a pilot with the Morane company, but was killed in a crash at Villacoublay on 10 July 1919.

Sous-Lieutenant Marcel Pierre Viallet, from Lyon, was almost 27 when the war began, and in his youth had seen much of the world. Back in France, he immediately joined the cavalry, but was badly wounded before 1914 was out. Requesting a transfer to aviation, Viallet had gained his wings by November 1915 and became a testing pilot on Caudrons. When finally able to join a frontline unit, he went to C53.

On 28 April Viallet and his observer attacked a Fokker *Eindecker* which they shot down, and two days later they drove off another fighter that was attacking a machine under their escort. Although their Caudron was badly shot about, Viallet managed to get it home. For these actions he received the *Médaille Militaire*. In June he was sent to N67 to fly Nieuports, and after a double victory on 6 August (one falling inside French lines), he was made a *Chevalier de la Légion d'Honneur* on the 29th. By the end of the year Viallet had achieved nine victories. Little is known of his later service, but after the war he remained in the military. Viallet contracted an illness during the Rif campaign in Morocco and died on 21 September 1925.

Pierre Pendaries ended the war with seven victories, three of which he scored with N69 between August 1916 and May 1917. Wounded whilst serving both with the army and the air service, he later flew with SPA67, flying in excess of 1100 hours in the defence of his country.

Escadrille N76 had Capitaine René Doumer as its principal ace, scoring five kills on Nieuports, which he added to two he had achieved with C64. From Laon, the 26-year-old had already seen service since 1908 in a *chasseur* battalion when war came. An infantry lieutenant, Doumer distinguished himself in action and became a *Chevalier de la Légion d'Honneur* on 17 September 1914, but had also been seriously wounded. Joining the air service, he flew Caudrons before going to a *chasse escadrille*. With seven official victories, Doumer fell in combat on 26 April 1917, shot down by Obltn Erich Hahn, leader of *Jasta* 19. His father had been Senator Paul Doumer, a later President of the *République*. Assassinated in Paris in 1932, Paul Doumer was honoured by the naming of a bridge in Hanoi in his memory. A future generation of American flyers would attack this bridge on numerous occasions during the Vietnam War.

N77's Maurice Boyau flew this highly decorated Nieuport 17 in 1917. He became an ace on the type, and later flying SPADs brought his tally to 35 before being shot down by Georg von Hantelmann of *Jasta* 15 on 16 September 1918 (*Greg VanWyngarden Collection*)

N76's insignia took the form of a triangular pennant facing aft, divided into equal sections of blue (forward) and yellow (aft).

Maurice Jean-Paul Boyau was another high-scoring fighter ace. Before his death in combat on 16 September 1918 (shot down by Georg von Hantelmann of *Jasta* 15), he had scored 35 victories. Born in Algeria in May 1888, he had been a pre-war soldier. After a period as a flying instructor, Boyau joined N77 in early 1917, and by the summer had ten victories. After the unit equipped with SPADs, his score

Leading N78, Capitaine Armand Pinsard had scored 16 victories on Nieuports during 1917 prior to being badly injured in an accident on 12 June. Having recovered by the following year, he returned to take command of SPA23, and ended the war with 27 victories. All this he achieved following his escape from a prison camp following his capture in February 1915 and his subsequent escape in March 1916

Capitaine Henri Hay de Slade became an ace flying Nieuports with N86, and by the end of the war he had scored 19 victories and was commanding SPA159

This Nieuport 27 (N5690), marked '12' in white, also features N87's arched-back cat emblem on its fuselage. The latter was applied in white, with a red collar, on camouflaged machines, and in black with a red collar on silver-doped scouts. N5690 was originally assigned to Sergent Marcel Gasser – who later scored ten victories while flying SPADs – before being passed on to Lt Marin. Gasser may have also scored one or two victories in Nieuports for N87 was operating a 'mixed bag' of types when he began scoring in the spring of 1918 (*via Jon Guttman*)

rose rapidly. Twenty-one of his claims were against balloons.

Capitaine Armand Pinsard was an air fighter with N78. Prior to World War 1 he had fought in Morocco with the *2nd Regiment de Spahis*, having joined the military in 1906 at age 19. Transferring to aviation in 1912, he was awarded the *Médaille Militaire* for actions during the great army manoeuvres in 1913. Assigned to MS23 on the outbreak of war, Pinsard was commissioned in November 1914, but on 8 February 1915 he was brought down and taken prisoner. He escaped and returned to France in April 1916. By July he was with N26, and in September he became a *Chevalier de la Légion d'Honneur* for six strafing attacks made on 7 August against German troops massing for a counter attack on French positions.

Pinsard gained his first victory on 1 November, and was then designated commander of N78. His second kill came on 23 January 1917, and by 5 June his tally had risen to 16. His scoring run was cut short by a serious crash on 12 June, but after several months in hospital, he returned to the front as commander of SPA23. By August 1918, now flying SPADs, Pinsard's score had risen to 27 and six probables. He was made an Officer of the *Légion d'Honneur*, having been cited in army orders more than a dozen times, and he also held the *Croix de Guerre* with 19 *Palmes*. Pinsard remained in the air force postwar, and in 1925 was made a Commander of the *Légion d'Honneur*, followed by a Grand Officer of the Order in December 1937.

In World War 2 Pinsard commanded fighter group *Groupe de Chasse 21*, but was severely injured in a bombing raid on 6 June 1940, losing a leg (see *Osprey Aircraft of the Aces 28 - French Aces of World War 2* for further details). He died in May 1953 during a dinner held by the flying veterans, *Les Vielles Tiges*, aged 66. N78's insignia was a black panther.

Capitaine Henri Joseph Marie Hay de Slade, from Brest, was 21 years old when the war started. An army cadet, he served with the cavalry prior to entering aviation, and saw his first war flying with N80 in 1916. The following spring he moved to N86, and by the end of the year was an ace. Once on SPADs, de Slade's score had risen to 11 by the time he was made CO of SPA59 in July 1918, bringing his tally to 19 by the Armistice. He was decorated by France, Britain and Italy, and lived until November 1979.

Marius Jean-Paul Elzeard Ambrogi (known as 'Marc') came from Marseilles, born in June 1895. After a short period in the army he moved to aviation, and flying with N90 he downed three German aircraft with the Nieuport, followed by a further 11 with SPADs. His 15th kill came in World War 2, when he shot down a Dornier bomber over France in a Bloch 152 before the surrender. Ambrogi died in April 1971.

Gustave Victorin Daladier was 26 when war broke out, and had been a soldier since 1907. Deciding to fly in 1915, he became a pilot. Flying with N93, he shot down four German two-seaters in 1917 and became an ace with a final tally of 12 kills once the unit had equipped with SPADs. Daladier died in April 1974.

Edmond Jacques Marcel Pillon was an NCO pilot with N102 and then N82. This 21-year-old first served in the infantry in 1914, and although he quickly moved to aviation, he did not become a pilot until 1916. With five victories by the summer of 1917, Pillon was then moved to SPA67 in 1918, adding two more kills before going to SPA98, where he claimed his eighth, and last, victory in September. Pillon was killed in a flying accident in June 1921.

Lt Gustav Daladier first flew with N73, but later, whilst flying with N93, scored at least four victories in 1917. He went on to become an ace with SPA93 in 1918, ending the war with 12 victories

Daladier's Nieuport 17 is surrounded by pilots from N93. The aircraft is marked with the *Escadrille's* distinctive black duck emblem, and also carries the individual number '4' (*via Jon Guttman*)

Sergent Edmund Pillon of N102 is seen flying his Nieuport on 24 December 1916. Having scored one victory with this unit, he was then posted to N82, where he became an ace. Pillon ended the war with eight kills, having claimed three further successes flying SPADs with SPAs 67 and 98 – he served as an adjudant with the latter unit. Pillon was killed in a flying accident in June 1921

Sergent André Lévy's Nieuport 17 (N2756) of N561 *Escadrille*. This unit flew on the Italian Front, charged with the defence of Venice. He gained six victories, several flying Nieuports, before becoming a prisoner of war during a balloon attack on 16 September 1918. The insignia is of a dog's head, and there also appears to be a dark ring marked around the rear edge of the cowling

Sous-Lieutenant Victor Francois Marie Alexis Regnier was a Nieuport ace with five victories. He joined the artillery in 1910 at the age of 21, serving for two years. Recalled at the outbreak of war, he was wounded in March 1915, and in the late summer joined the air service. Initially serving with a bombing squadron, he transferred to N112, and fighters, being commissioned on 10 September 1916. After gaining his fifth victory Regnier was severely wounded in combat. He did not see further frontline service, but remained in the military until war's end, despite a bad crash in August 1918. He had been made a *Chevalier de la Légion d'Honneur* and held the *Croix de Guerre* with four *Palmes* and two *Etoiles de Vermeil*. Like Pinsard, Regnier too saw service in World War 2, and was made a Commander of the *Légion d'Honneur*.

André Robert Lévy came from Paris, born in June 1893, and saw the first war years in the trenches. After pilot training he was sent to Italy to fly Nieuports with N561, charged with the defence of Venice. With this

unit he scored six victories before he was shot down and captured during a balloon attack on 16 September 1918. Lévy died in 1973.

Lafayette Escadrille

As the United States of America did not come into the war until April 1917, there were many US citizens who wished to fight for the Allies, and any number joined the RFC, often via Canada. Others, either because of ties with France, or simply because France was 'where the action was', sailed directly to that country to enlist. For them to be able to fight, they first had to join the French *Foreign Legion*, but then those who felt a desire to fly were able to apply to transfer into aviation.

As there were so many Americans keen to fight for the Allies, some thought it a good idea that they should be grouped together as a squadron, but this posed political difficulties, especially when it was decided to call it the *Escadrille Americaine.* This was later changed to *Escadrille* N124, but the unit was popularly known as the *Lafayette Escadrille.* It came at a time when romantic notions of war had yet to be sullied by reality, but nevertheless, the concept caught the imagination of both the French and American public, and many other US citizens joined the French Air Service.

Indeed, the response was so great that there were too many for one unit, so selected volunteers went into what was called the *Lafayette* Flying Corps, with new pilots going to other regular French *escadrilles* as vacancies arose. Many from both the *escadrille* and the corps later transferred into the American Air Service once this became established in France in early 1918.

Although the N124 pilots had their share of successes, being led by a Frenchman with two French flight commanders, only one ace was produced – Raoul Lufbery. Gervais Raoul Lufbery was in fact born in France, the third son of a New York chemist and a French mother who had met in Paris while the former was working as a chemist for a local chocolate firm. However, his mother died before Raoul reached his first birthday. Remarrying, Lufbery senior returned to the US, leaving his sons in France.

Raoul Lufbery stands in front of his camouflaged Nieuport 11 (N1256) in late 1916, cradling one of N124's canine mascots in his arms (*via Greg VanWyngarden*)

Raoul Lufbery's silver-doped Nieuport 21 N1615 which he flew whilst serving with the *Lafayette Escadrille* at Bar-le-Duc in September 1916 (*via Jon Guttman*)

In his youth, Raoul saw much of the world, even going to America in 1906-08, before joining the American army. Later, he travelled once more, meeting, in 1912, the French aviator Marc Pourpe, and eventually becoming his mechanic. When the war began Pourpe joined the air service and so did Lufbery, via the *Legion*, serving as a mechanic. However, after Pourpe was killed in a crash, Lufbery decided to become a pilot in order to avenge his friend's death.

Assigned to VB106 from October 1915 to May 1916, he tried to get onto fighters but 'washed out' and almost returned to bombers. However, he passed his tests and was the eighth official member of N124. After many sorties and more than a dozen combats, Lufbery scored his first victory on 30 July, a second the next day and a third on 4 August. Four days later came number four, which gained for him the *Médaille Militaire* to add to his *Croix de Guerre*.

Lufbery became the first American ace whilst flying with the French by shooting down a Roland two-seater on 12 October 1916, and he was promoted to adjudant. By the end of the year he had six kills, plus several

This Nieuport 17 was also flown by Lufbery, and it wears the *Lafayette's* original 'Seminole' Indian head insignia and three 'coup' bars on the fuselage

more unconfirmed, and throughout 1917 he added regularly to his score so that by the end of that year he had achieved 16 (possibly 17) victories. Lufbery had also received the *Légion d'Honneur*, the British Military Medal and at least ten *Palmes* to his war cross. In addition, he received the Medal for Military Valour from Montenegro.

Edwin C Parsons flew both with *Escadrille Lafayette* and SPA3

Transferring to the US Air Service, Lufbery was given the rank of major and made commander of the 94 Aero Squadron, flying Nieuport 28s. He had two unconfirmed victories in April 1918, but on 19 May, flying Nieuport 28 N6178, he took off to intercept a two-seater but the observer's fire set his machine ablaze and he jumped from the burning machine, falling into a garden in the village of Maron, north of Nancy. At the time of death he officially had at least 13 probables to his name, although his companions in the *Lafayette* think the actual figure was much higher – it simply did not bother Lufbery that he did not have distant combat successes confirmed.

William 'Bill' Thaw did not achieve ace status with N124, but with two kills, followed by three more with the American 103rd Aero, he did so eventually. In addition he had at least three probables with the French. Born in Pittsburgh, Pennsylvania, in August 1893, he had learned to fly pre-war, while at Yale. Thaw's father later bought him a Curtiss Hydro flying boat, and taking the machine to France to compete in the Schnei-

Edwin Parsons' *Lafayette* Nieuport 17 (or 21) is seen in 1916 after Kenneth Marr overshot on landing and ended up on a railway embankment by the airfield

der Trophy races, he handed it over to the French when war was declared. He then enlisted and saw duty in the trenches.

Finally able to transfer to aviation, Thaw served as an observer in D6 and then as a corporal pilot with C42 in 1915. Once N124 was being formed, he managed a transfer, via a brief stay with N65, and gained his first victory on 24 May 1916 – a Fokker *Eindecker*. When he left to transfer to the US Air Service at the end of 1917, he had received the *Croix de Guerre* with four *Palmes* and two *Stars*, plus the *Légion d'Honneur*. Once N124 became the 103rd Aero, he took command and won the Distinguished Service Cross for downing a balloon on 20 April, followed by a German fighter, which made him an ace. Thaw later added an Oak Leaf Cluster (Bar) to this decoration. Postwar, retiring as a lieutenant-colonel, he went into civil aviation in Pittsburgh, but died of pneumonia in April 1934, aged 40.

N124's Bill Thaw stands by his Nieuport 17 N1582, which was fitted with a *cône de penetration*. Note the flying helmet hanging on the wing bracing wires (*via Greg VanWyngarden*)

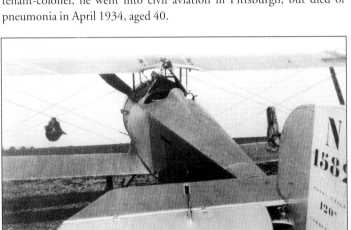

Another view of Bill Thaw's Nieuport 17 N1582, marked with the letter 'T'. Note the two rear-view mirrors, one on the trailing edge of the upper wing centre section and the other on the right side of the cockpit sill (*via Jon Guttman*)

This photograph of N1582 reveals the gun mounting and the *cône de penetration*

OTHER ALLIED ACES

Belgian Air Service

Belgium, with more than half of its homeland under German occupation, nevertheless had its own air force in action throughout the war, and helped defend the line across Belgium with the North Sea on its left flank. Flying French and British aeroplanes, its gallant, but small band of aviators saw much action. Belgian aces were necessarily few in number, but like the French they only counted confirmed victories in a pilot's score, (destroyed, not even forced to land damaged or otherwise) and also counted shared kills.

Andre Emile Alfons de Meulemeester came from Bruges, volunteering for aviation soon after war began. Assigned to the Belgian *1 ère Escadrille* in October 1916, he was known as Sgt 'Mystére'. His first claim which was not confirmed came on 1 February 1917. His first official victory was scored on 30 April, this success being shared with the British pilot of a Sopwith Scout. Victory number two was scored on 12 June with Sergent G Kervyn de Lettenhove. Two more kills came in July and number five went down on 21 August, although de Meulemeester was wounded during the latter engagement. His sixth Nieuport victory was scored on 4 November, again with de Lettenhove.

Later flying Hanriots with the *escadrille* and with *9 ère*, de Meulemeester ended the war with 11 official and 17 unofficial victories. He had been injured in a crash on 11 July 1918, which cost him some teeth, but he survived the war as a *Chevalier de l'Ordre Leopold*, and having been awarded the *Croix de Guerre* with *Palme*, five citations from the Belgian and French, six *Chevrons de front* and one *Chevron de blessure*, together

1 ére Escadrille's **Andre de Meulemeester (left) and Georges 'Jojo' Kervyn de Lettenhove stand by the former's Nieuport 23 N3625. De Meulemeester scored seven victories on Nieuports and four on Hanriots, whilst de Lettenhove claimed four confirmed successes (and nine probables). The Nieuport marked with the name *VAMPIRE* in the background was flown by both Henri 'Riri' Crombez and de Lettenhove** (*Aviation Society of Antwerp*)

Jan Olieslagers, sat in the cockpit of
a Nieuport 16 fitted with twin Lewis
guns. He scored four confirmed
victories on Nieuports and two on
Hanriots (*Bruce/Leslie collection*)

with the French *Croix de Guerre* and Italian *Medaglio d'Argento al Valore Militaire*. After the war de Meulemeester went into the family brewery business and never flew again. He died in his home town on 7 March 1973, aged 79.

Lt Jean Olieslagers, known as the 'Antwerp Devil', had been a motor-bike rider pre-war, becoming World Champion in 1902 when he was 19. In 1909 he bought a Blériot monoplane and learnt to fly (Belgian brevet No 5), and between 1910-13 he took seven world flying records. When war came the Germans even asked for his help with aerial observation!

Olieslagers runs the engine up on a
2 ére Escadrille Nieuport two-seater
which has been converted into a
single-seat scout
(*Aviation Society of Antwerp*)

Joining the Belgian Air Service, Olieslagers became its first fighter pilot to claim a victory in air combat flying a Nieuport 10 with *2 ére*, on 12 September 1915 – an Aviatik two-seater. Although this was a 'forced to land' victory, it was made official. He scored two more unofficial victories on the Nieuport 10 before the end of the year, then went to *1 ére*, where he again flew Nieuport 10s and, later, 11s Olieslagers rarely took claiming seriously, but officialdom ruled that by June 1917, when the *Escadrille* began to fly Hanriot Scouts, Olieslagers had four official and at least a dozen unofficial kills, with at least one of the latter not being confirmed merely because there had been no officer present to witness the aeroplane's fall! With the Hanriot he became an ace – officially – but his six victories seem small measure considering his prolonged time in combat. For instance, in 1916 alone Olieslagers flew 193 patrols and engaged in 52 combats, whilst in 1918 he flew 141 sorties and had at least 15 combats.

He was made a *Chevalier de l'Ordre Leopold* and received the *Croix de Guerre* with *Palme, Croix de l'Yser du Feu, Médaille du Volontaire Combattant* 1914-18 and eight *Chevrons de front*. Olieslagers was also awarded the French *Legion d'Honneur*, French *Croix de Guerre*, Russian St Stanislaus Order, and Serbian Golden Medal.

Sous-Lieutenant Edmond Thieffry came from Etterbeck, near Brussels, and had just become a lawyer when the war started. He immediately became a prisoner of war, but escaped and became a pilot – although not a very good one, judging by the number of crashes he sustained. Thieffry nevertheless persevered, and perhaps for the preservation of observers, flew single-seaters! Flying with *5 ére*, he scored his first confirmed victory on 15 March 1917 and his second eight days later. He 'made ace' on 3 July in a combat which saw him become the first Belgian to score a double victory – two German Marine Albatros D III scouts north of Dixmude.

Thieffry's *escadrille* then received SPADs as their equipment, and he scored four more victories on these before being shot down on 23 February 1918, attacking a two-seater of *Flieger Abteilung* 227. Wounded, and in a German hospital in Ghent, he had at least survived and in April he

Edmund Thieffry flew this Nieuport 23 during his service with *5 ére Escadrille*. The comet motif which adorns this fighter was the unit emblem. Thieffry scored six victories on Nieuports and four on SPADs

Future top-scoring Belgian ace Willy Coppens sits in his Nieuport marked with his personal emblem before the 'thistle' insignia denoted *Escadrille 9 me*. **The marking seen in this photograph was later used by** *Escadrille 11 me*. **Most of Coppens' 37 victories were scored on the Hanriot (***via Walter Pieters***)**

managed to escape, but was soon retaken. After the war he returned to law and also took up politics, but his love of flying had not diminished and in early 1925 he and two companions flew an aeroplane to the Belgian Congo. The trio did much flying in the Congo, but on 11 April 1929 the aeroplane was caught in a tropical storm and crashed. Thieffry and one of his friends were killed. He was 36, and left a wife and five children. During the war he had been made a *Chevalier de l'Ordre Leopold* and also received the *Croix de Guerre*. After his death he was made an *Officier de l'Ordre Leopold* for his pioneering work in Africa.

US Air Service

American fighter units arriving in France at the beginning of 1918 had no aeroplanes, and therefore had to rely on machines from both the RFC and French Air Service. Two US squadrons attached to the British had Sopwith Camels (17th and 148th) whilst the rest, operating with the French, were given Nieuport 28s.

Oddly enough the French themselves had rejected this machine in favour of the SPAD XIII, but in early 1918 there were not enough SPADs to loan to the Americans, so they gave them the rejected Type '28'. The first two US Aero Squadrons to equip were the 94th and 95th, although initially the aircraft arrived without guns. Both units were prepared for combat by March, however when it was realised the pilots of the 95th had not received adequate gunnery training they were pulled out until early May.

The Type 28 was a very different looking aeroplane in comparison with previous Nieuports. It had a longer fuselage for one thing, and it did not have the familiar sesquiplane wing configuration, nor the famous 'V' struts, although the cowling was similar and its rudder was modelled on the tail surface of the Nieuport 27. The two machine guns were fitted on the port side of the cowling in an unusual attitude different from any other Allied, or German, fighter type.

American pilots flew their first patrols in unarmed Type 28s, this curious arrangement being undertaken simply for morale purposes, so obviously pilots did not have orders to cross the lines. As guns began to arrive, they were issued one to an aircraft, the second one being fitted as supplies were stepped up. The first combat action came on 14 April 1918, with two German pilots of *Jasta* 64 falling to Alan Winslow and Douglas Campbell of the 94th. As 1918 progressed, two new squadrons, the 27th and 147th joined the 94th and 95th to form the 1st Pursuit Group.

Despite some lack of overall confidence in the Type 28 – it had a tendency to shed wing fabric in a dive pull-out and an engine that might catch fire if a pilot forgot to cut his petrol flow when shutting off his ignition on landing – the American pilots didn't do too badly. By July SPAD

XIIIs were beginning to arrive, and the transition was complete by the start of August. However, during the units' brief period with the Nieuport, a handful of Americans had achieved ace status.

Lt Douglas Campbell of the 94th became the first American-trained pilot to down five German aircraft. From California, born in June 1896, this Harvard and Cornell Universities man gained his first victory on 14 April 1918, and by 31 May had become an ace. He added a

sixth on 5 June, but was wounded in the action, fighting on despite a bullet lodged in his back. Campbell's period in combat earned him the DSC with four Oak Leaf Clusters, *Légion d'Honneur* and *Croix de Guerre* with two *Palmes*. Five of his six confirmed claims came whilst flying N6158, marked '0', and in which David Peterson had claimed two earlier victories. Campbell returned to France in late 1918, too late to see combat again. In the 1930s he was with Pan American Airways, becoming a vice president in 1939 and general manager in 1948. He died in December 1990 aged 94.

David McKelvey Peterson, from Pennsylvania, born July 1894, had joined the French in 1916 and had seen duty with the *Lafayette Escadrille*, gaining one victory in September 1917. Once he transferred to the USAS in February 1918, flying with the 103rd Aero (formally N124), he was

Douglas Campbell, of the 94th Aero, became the first all-American trained fighter pilot to become an ace with the US Air Service. He is seen standing by his Nieuport 28 'white 10' (N6164) in which he scored his first victory on 14 April 1918 (*via Greg VanWyngarden*)

Eddie Rickenbacker, Doug Campbell and Ken Marr (CO of the 94th Aero). Note the white paint on the central area of the Nieuport's propeller, cowling and wheel struts (*via Greg VanWyngarden*)

David Peterson claimed six victories on Nieuports, scoring one with N124, three with the 94th Aero and two with the 95th. He was killed in a flying accident in Florida on 16 March 1919

James Meissner of the 94th Aero stands alongside his battered '14' (N6144), having struggled back to his airfield after the Nieuport 28 had shed its upper wing fabric on 2 May 1918. Note the 'Liberty' poster stuck to the upper surface of the fighter's lower wing. On this day Meissner had been involved in his first combat, shooting down a Hannover C-type. He scored four victories with the 94th and four more with the 147th, flying SPADs (*via Greg VanWyngarden*)

then made a flight commander with the 94th. Flying Nieuport 28s Peterson claimed five more victories and was promoted to major in August. He received the DSC with Oak Leaf Cluster as well as the French *Croix de Guerre*. Returning home after the war Peterson was killed in a flying accident at Daytona Beach, Florida, in March 1919.

James Armand Meissner, from Brooklyn, New York (born Nova Scotia 20 July 1896) was another Cornell graduate. Assigned to the 94th in March 1918, he was lucky to survive his first combat. Fabric from the top wing of his Nieuport (N6144 '14') ripped away in a dive on 2 May shortly after he had shot down his first victory – a Hannover CL two-seater – but he managed to land without further injury to his machine, or to himself. On 30 May Meissner had another narrow escape, colliding with an Albatros Scout during a fight, but again he was able to get his damaged Nieuport (N6144, now marked '8') down safely. He received the DSC and an Oak Leaf cluster, and was also awarded the *Croix de Guerre* from the French. With four confirmed victories, Meissner was given command of the 147th Aero and downed his fifth victory on 1 August. Flying SPADs, he added another three kills to his tally, ending the war with eight. Postwar, Meissner helped form and organise the Alabama National Guard, and at one stage was its CO. He died on 16 January 1936, aged 39.

The top-scoring American pilot to fly with the USAS was Edward Vernon Rickenbacker. Eddie Rickenbacker was no youngster, being 27 (born October 1890). From Columbus, Ohio, 'Rick' had been a pre-war racing driver, and tested cars. Going to England in 1916 with the automobile industry, he decided to 'join the colours', and was at one stage a driver with the

rank of sergeant. Deciding on a more active role, Rickenbacker transferred to the Air Service, and after training joined the 94th Aero in March 1918. He gained his first combat victory on 29 April (N6159 '12'), and by the end of May had made ace with five official victories and a sixth which was not officially confirmed until 1960! Most of his Nieuport claims were in N6169 marked '1'.

Going down with an ear infection, by the time Rickenbacker returned to the 94th in September it had equipped with SPADs, and during the final weeks of the war he brought his score to 26. He ended with war as a captain with the DSC and nine Oak Leaf clusters, the *Croix de Guerre* with three *Palmes*, and had been made a *Chevalier de la Légion d'Honneur*. Twelve years later he was awarded his country's highest decoration for heroism in the field with the Medal of Honor. After the war Rickenbacker set up a car business and then went into aviation. He remained in the public eye until his death in July 1973, in Zurich, Switzerland, aged 82.

Italian Air Force

The air war fought over north and north-eastern Italy against the forces of the Austro-Hungarians was very different from that waged on the Western Front in France. However, the Italian fighter force, while it comprised several different aeroplane types, did for some while fly a variety of Nieuports. Apart from a few machines purchased directly from France, most were built under licence by Nieuport-Macchi. However, as the war progressed the Italian Air Service gradually went over to SPADs and Hanriots.

Nevertheless, several Nieuport 11s, 17s and 27s were used by aces, and while most of the pilots who saw action in 1918 were flying the Hanriot,

America's 'ace of aces', Capt Eddie Rickenbacker. Flying Nieuport 28s with the 94th Aero, he had claimed six victories before an ear infection took him away from the Front. Returning to fly SPADs with the 94th, his tally had risen to 26 by war's end, although it took until 1960 for the 26th kill to be confirmed!
(*via Greg VanWyngarden*)

Doug Campbell poses in front of Type 28 N6179 'white 11', which was usually flown by Reed Chambers with the 94th Aero (*via Greg VanWyngarden*)

A future SPAD 13 ace Reed Chambers stands alongside Nieuport 28 'white 11'

a number had already achieved ace status on the Nieuport, while others had begun their scoring careers on the type.

Maggiore Francesco Baracca was the leading Italian ace in World War 1. Born in Lugo di Romagna in the province of Ravenna, he was in his late 20s during his most prolific scoring period at the front. Born in May 1888, he saw duty with the cavalry pre-war but volunteered to fly in 1912. Commissioned, Baracca went to Paris in 1915 to convert to Nieuport Scouts, returning to fly Nieuport 10s with *1ª Squadriglia*. However, the Type 11 soon proved the better machine, and he used one to down his first opponent on 7 April 1916, which was also the first official Italian victory of the war.

With three victories, Baracca moved to *70ª Squadriglia* that summer, and by April 1917 he had achieved eight kills. He then joined *91ª Squadriglia*, flying both Nieuports and SPADs before settling on SPAD VIIs and XIIIs. By June 1918 he had scored 34 victories and won his country's top honours including a Gold Medal for Military Valour and three Silver Medals. Baracca had also been made an Officer of the Military Order of Savoy, and had received the British Military Cross, French *Croix de Guerre* with *Palmes*, the Gold Cross from Serbia and the Officer's Cross of the Belgian Crown. He fell in action on 19 June 1918 during a strafing sortie, the cause of death still remaining unclear to this day.

Flavio Torello Baracchini achieved 21 victories before being wounded in June 1918, eight of these kills being gained whilst flying with *81ª Squadriglia*. From Villafranca Lunigiana, born in July 1895, he was with the engineers in the early part of the war. Once he had learnt to fly Baracchini saw service with a Voisin squadron, and following conversion to

Francesco Baracca and his Nieuport 11 N1431 of *1ª Squadriglia* are seen in the spring of 1916. The aircraft was clear-doped overall, with 'dark' border tapes. Baracca went on to become Italy's 'ace of aces' with 34 kills, flying Nieuports and SPADs. He adopted a black prancing horse as his personal insignia. Flying later with *70ª* and *91ª Squadriglia*, many of his early victories were scored flying Nieuports prior to the arrival of SPADs. Baracca was killed in action on 19 June 1918 (*via Greg VanWyngarden*)

Seen at far right, six-kill ace Luigi Olivi served as CO of *76ª Squadriglia* in 1916-17. Standing alongside him is General Novelli and his son Tenente Gastone Novelli, who scored at least three victories with Nieuports flying with *81ª* and *91ª Squadriglia* in 1917-18 – his final tally was eight. Novelli was killed in a flying accident in July 1919 (*via G Alegi*)

Nieuports, joined *81ª Squadriglia*. In the summer of 1917 he began to fly the Hanriot with *76ª Squadriglia*, adding four more kills to his tally, then returned to *81ª*. Now flying Hanriots as well, Baracchini brought his score to 21, although it could have been as high as 33, before a wound ended his combat career. After the war he worked in a chemical laboratory, but was badly burned in an explosion on 29 July 1928 and died in Rome the following August.

Sergente Marziale Cerutti came from Brescia, born in March 1895. He served with the artillery before flight training, and eventually ended up with *79ª Squadriglia* flying Nieuport Scouts. His first three claims in 1917 were not confirmed, but success finally came on 24 November and he became an ace on 28 January 1918 with two kills shared with another pilot (Reali). Cerutti's ace of clubs-marked Nieuport 11, and later a Type 27, also had the initials 'MIR' on the side, which stood for *Marziale Imperatore Romano* (Martial of the Roman Emperor). His last three official victories went down on 27 October 1918, whilst flying his Nieuport 27. Cerutti received three Silver Medals, the French *Croix de Guerre* and the Serbian Star of Karageorgevic with Swords. He was commissioned in 1919.

After the war Cerutti joined the *Regia Aeronautica*, and by 1931 he was a group commander. In 1935-36 he was CO of *15°* and then *11° Stormo*. During World War 2 Cerutti saw duty in North Africa, and in 1941 was a *generale di Brigata Area*, and in August was appointed Chief of Staff of Transport Command. Having survived two world wars, Marziale Cerutti died in a motorcycle crash in May 1946.

Sergente Attilio Imolesi, from Cesena, was aged 26 when he joined *79ª Squadriglia*. He is believed to have scored all of his victories on Nieuports, between August 1917 and January 1918, although his first unconfirmed claims came in April 1917. He was awarded a Silver and Bronze Medal before being injured in a crash near Marostica on 11 March 1918.

Tenente Carlo Francesco Lombardi was born in Genoa in January 1897. Following duty with the infantry, he learnt to fly, and with *77ª Squadriglia* gained five (possibly six) of his eight victories flying Nieuports. He received three Silver Medals. Postwar, Lombardi worked for the family rice refinery, but he continued his interest in flying and was well known for his record-breaking flights, and for forming the Avia aviation company in 1938. He died in March 1983.

Tenente Luigi Olivi, born Campobasso in November 1894, lived in Ancona pre-war and learnt to fly between 1914-15. Injured in a crash in October 1915, following a speedy recovery he joined *2ª Squadriglia*, where he undertook artillery co-operation duties. Converting to Nieuports, Olivi was assigned to *76ª Squadriglia* in July 1916. He claimed eight victories, of which six were officially confirmed, the last one on 17 June 1917. It was whilst returning to photograph the wreckage of this kill that he was shot down and killed near Moraro. Olivi had received two Silver Medals.

Tenente-Colonnello Pier Ruggero Piccio was born in Rome in 1880 and had been in the infantry pre-war, seeing service in Africa, Crete and Libya, before becoming a pilot in 1913. He flew recce sorties when Italy came into the war and commanded a bomber squadron. Later flying Nieuports, Piccio served as CO of *77™* and then *91ª Squadriglias*, and later still commanded *10° Gruppo*. In all he scored 24 victories, plus oth-

Pier Ruggero Piccio (centre) gained 23 of his 24 victories flying with *91ª Squadriglia* in 1917-18, with possibly as many as ten kills obtained on Nieuports. He ended the war with the rank of lieutenant-colonel, commanding a fighter group (*via Greg VanWyngarden*)

This portrait of Pier Piccio was taken some years after World War 1

ers unconfirmed, and although he flew different aircraft, he downed at least five with the Nieuport. Piccio was awarded two Silver and one Gold Medals, and an Officer's Cross in the Military Order of Savoy.

After the war Piccio was air attaché in Paris, and in 1923 he was made honorary ADC to the King of Italy. By December 1923 he was a generale, and AOC (later Chief of Staff) of the *Regia Aeronautica*. Following another tour in Paris between 1927-33, he became a Senator. Following World War 2 Piccio resided mostly in France, but died in Rome in July 1965.

Tenente Ferruccio Ranza was an engineer when war started, but the 22-year-old joined the aviation service in 1915, going to *43ª Squadriglia* to fly recce missions. He won the Bronze Medal in 1916 but then converted to Nieuports and was sent to *77ª Squadriglia*. Flying Nieuport 11s, Ranza claimed six victories (four being confirmed) before being posted to *91ª Squadriglia*. His fifth victory came on 23 June. Ranza continued to score steadily during 1917, having increased his tally to 12 victories by the end of the year. A further five victories followed in 1918, flying SPADs, and during this year he took command of the *squadriglia*.

Ranza received three Silver Medals and was Knighted in the Military Order of Savoy. His foreign awards comprised four War Crosses, including French and Belgian, plus the Serbian Star of Karageogevich. Remaining in the air force postwar, Ranza climbed the ranks to become AOC in Tripolitania, and was later AOC of Italian East Africa in 1935. Promoted to *generale di Brigata Aerea* in 1935, he later became AOC in Albania in 1939 and in Southern Italy in 1940. Ranza retired in early 1945 and died in Bologna in April 1973.

Sergente Antonio Reali, from Torino Province, was born in March 1891 and first saw service as an engineer. Learning to fly in 1915, and going on to Nieuports, he was assigned to *79ª Squadriglia* in early 1917. Although he made early claims, he did not gain a confirmed success until 14 January 1918, but by war's end had achieved 11 victories, as well as 18 unconfirmed claims. Reali had become an ace in less than a month flying Nieuports, and won the Silver Medal. He left the service in 1919, but rejoined the *Regia Aeronautica* reserve in 1923, becoming a capitano at the end of 1940. Reali died in January 1975.

Sergente Cosimo Rizzotto, was born in June 1893 and was an airman pre-war before volunteering for flight training. Assigned to the *77ª Squadriglia*, he was credited with five victories on Nieuports in 1917 and one flying a SPAD in 1918. Awarded two Silver Medals, he emigrated to South America postwar, becoming an instructor in both Argentina and Paraguay. Rizzotto died in Milan in February 1963.

Tenente Fulco Ruffo di Calabria came from Napoli, born on 12 August 1884. From a military family, he became a cavalry officer pre-war. Learning to fly at the beginning of the war, he flew two-seaters until transferred to fighters after winning two Bronze Medals. Posted to *1ª Squadriglia*, di Calabria gained his first victory on 23 August 1916, and a month later he joined *70ª Squadriglia*. His score began to rise in 1917, especially when sent to *91ª Squadriglia*, and he achieved perhaps nine victories on Nieuports. Di Calabria 'made ace' on 5 May. Later flying SPADs, he had raised his score to 20 by war's end. Di Calabria had received another Bronze Medal, the Silver Medal and then a Gold.

Fulco Ruffo di Calabria and his personal insignia. Flying with *1ª*, *70ª* and *91ª Squadriglias*, he had achieved 20 victories by mid-June 1918, with at least eight of these being scored on Nieuport Scouts

He became CO of the *Squadriglia* after Baracca's death, but suffered a break down. He returned to command *10° Gruppo* in October, but was shot down by AA fire. Di Calabria was Knighted to the Military Order of Savoy, and although he nominally remained in service, reaching the rank of tenente-colonnello in 1942, he had virtually retired to manage his estates at Paliano. He died on 23 August 1946. He was famous for his black skull and crossbones insignia on his aeroplanes.

Tenente Giovanni Sabelli, from Napoli, born in September 1886, had learnt to fly at Brooklands, in England, in 1912, so it was natural for him to join the Italian air service when war began. He became a very

This Macchi-built Nieuport 11 (N1685) was flown by Fulco Ruffo di Calabria of *70ª Squadriglia* in January 1917. The black skull and crossbones on the clear doped fuselage was his personal marking. Although not clearly visible in this photograph, the fighter mounted an unusual Colt machine-gun on the top wing (*A Casirati/P Moncalvo via Greg VanWyngarden*)

Sergente Mario Stoppani scored six victories flying Nieuport 11s with *76ª Squadriglia* in 1916. He is seen here seated in N1673, the fighter being fitted with a rear-view mirror on the central wing strut and some kind of sighting device stuck onto the windscreen itself (*via G Alegi*)

experienced Nieuport pilot, for in 1916 he served with the *2ª Squadriglia*, winning a Silver Medal despite no confirmed victories being achieved, and then flew as a Nieuport test pilot. Sabelli then commanded the Nieuport Defence Section in Albania until February 1917. After a brief stay with *71ª Squadriglia*, he went to *91ª*. In the summer of 1917 he achieved five victories, which earned him another Silver Medal. However, on 25 October Sabelli was shot down in flames attacking a two-seater over Bainsizza.

Tenente Silvio Scaroni, from Brescia, born in May 1893, was a former artillery man who learnt to fly in 1915. Assigned to an artillery co-operation unit, he won the Bronze Medal, and then flew reconnaissance missions, gaining a Silver Medal. Converting to Nieuports, he joined *76ª Squadriglia*. Although his first combat target was seen to crash behind the enemy lines, Scaroni made no claim, but by the middle of December he had achieved six victories. The unit was then equipped mainly with Hanriots, and with this type he raised his score to 26 by July 1918. He had received a second Silver Medal on Nieuports, and in 1918 came the Gold. However, he was badly wounded on 13 July and saw no further combat.

Nieuport 11 N1650 was flown by Mario Stoppani in late 1916, although this is clearly not him sat on the fuselage decking. Note the red, white and green fuselage bands aft of the cockpit (*via G Alegi*)

Postwar, Scaroni was with the Italian Aeronautical Mission to Argentina, but left the service in January 1920. Returning to duty as a regular officer, he was air attaché to Britain in 1924-25, the United States between 1925-30 and then went to China in 1935-37 as Head of the Italian Aviation Mission. A generale in World War 2, Scaroni was AOC of the *Aeronautica della Sicilia* between 1941-43 prior to his retirement in 1943. He died in Milan in February 1977.

Sergente Mario Stoppani scored six victories on Nieuport 11s in 1916. Born near Bergamo in May 1895, he had been an auto mechanic pre-war. He enlisted in the air service in 1913 but was not allowed to volunteer for flight training until 1915. After his six victories with *76ª Squadriglia*, and being awarded two Silver Medals, Stoppani joined Ansaldo aviation, in Genoa, as the company test pilot. After the war he became an instructor at Foggia, and then in Passignano in 1925, with SAI. He then resumed test piloting duties for SISA airline for 16 years, before becoming chief test pilot for Cant. During his career Stoppani made 15 first flights and set 41 world flying records. After World War 2 he worked for Breda and then SIAI Marchetti. He died in September 1959.

Imperial Russian Air Service

The Imperial Russian Air Service had its origins formulated in 1910, and its main equipment was French-built aeroplanes. Within four years its apparent size seemed impressive, but many of its aircraft were far from new and had not been well maintained. When the war with Germany began, Russian airmen commenced operations with aircraft that would, for the most part, still be in service well into 1916. Aeroplanes from Russian companies were slow in coming, which resulted in the air service relying heavily on French equipment.

Nieuport two-seaters (Types 10 and 12) were among the French purchases, along with fighter types like the 11 and, later, the 17. Some were camouflaged in green and brown while others retained their French silver finish. As the war progressed, more up-to-date types appeared too, such as Nieuport 21s and 23s.

Seen seated on the wheel of his Nieuport 10 '222', Maj A A Kozakov was Russia's 'ace of aces' during World War 1. He scored 19 of his 20 victories in Type 10s, 11s and 17s between June 1916 and October 1917. Kozakov was killed when his Sopwith Snipe crashed on 1 August 1919 (*via Greg VanWyngarden*)

This Nieuport 16 is finished in clear-dope overall, with Russian cockades in multiple positions (*via Greg VanWyngarden*)

It is difficult to write anything about the Russian fighter units without the end result feeling inadequate in comparison with the huge, and valuable, book *The Imperial Russian Air Service* by Alan Durkota *et al* (Flying Machines Press, 1995) so I shan't, but will refer the reader to this volume instead.

At the end of 1916 there were 12 Fighter Detachments, and while they flew a variety of equipment, the Nieuports were well to the fore prior to the eventual arrival of SPADs, but even then Nieuports continued in action until the time of the Revolution at the end of 1917.

Pilot claim credits were based on similar ideas to the French, shared victories being acknowledged as long as confirmation was established. Sometimes too, it was enough to 'defeat' the opposing aeroplane rather than destroy it. There were also a number of Russian pilots who saw duty with the French in France, just as a number of French pilots had periods of action on the Russian front.

In fact, the first ace on the Russian Front, if one merely counts his score, was a man who claimed his first four victories in France. Eduard Martynovich Pulpe had been born in Latvia in 1880 and had studied at Moscow University. Learning to fly in France in 1912, it was natural for him to join the French Air Service when war came, and his first two claims were made over Verdun in 1915 flying a Morane with MS23. In 1916 Pulpe scored twice more with his *escadrille*, which now flew Nieuports as N23. Awarded the *Médaille Militaire* and *Croix de Guerre*, he proceeded to Russia in the late spring of 1917, and flying with the 10th Detachment in a Nieuport 11, shot down his fifth victim on 1 July. On 2 August he was shot down by a two-seater crew, the pilot being future German ace, Erwin Bˆhme, and he succumbed to his injuries. Pulpe received a posthumous Order of St George, 4th Class.

The first all-Russian ace – and all scored in Russia – was Aleksandr Aleksandrovich Kozakov, who would also be the Russian top scorer in World War 1. Born in January 1889, he had been a cavalryman pre-war and transferred to aviation in 1913. Flying a Morane with the 4th Air Corps Detachment in Poland, he gained his first victory on 31 March 1915 – by ramming! For his daring actions he received the Order of St Anne, 4th Class, and then the 3rd Class. In September Kozakov moved to the 19th Corps Detachment and took command. Flying Nieuport 10s and 11s he became an ace on 21 December.

By the time he began flying the Nieuport 17 in mid-May 1917, Kozakov had achieved eight victories, and his score had risen to 20 by 26 October. He resigned his commission in January 1918 after the Revolution, and later joined the Slavo-British flying detachment against the Bolsheviks. When the British forces finally decided to withdraw and the White forces were fast losing the conflict, Kozakov took to the air in a Sopwith Snipe on the evening of 1 August 1919 and appeared to deliberately stall and crash, being killed on impact.

Capitaine Paul Vladimirovich d'Argueff was born in Yalta, Crimea, on 1 March 1887. He completed his training at the military academy in Odessa in 1907 and saw duty as an infantry officer. On detachment in France he first saw action on the Western Front but was wounded on 23 September 1914, and again in April 1915. With the *Croix de Guerre*, and then made a *Chevalier de la Légion d'Honneur*, d'Argueff received a wound on 2 May that made him unfit for frontline service, so he transferred to aviation.

After brief service with N48, d'Argueff transferred to Russia and to the 19th Fighter Detachment. Gaining his first victory on 10 January 1917, he had achieved six kills on Nieuport Scouts by 20 June. In 1918 he returned to France and flew SPADs with SPA124, bringing his score to 15 by war's end. Finding employment as an airline pilot postwar, d'Argueff was killed in a bad-weather crash on the German-Czech border on 30 October 1922.

Juri Vladimirovich Gilsher was from the Russian nobility, born in Moscow in November 1894. His desire to become a civil engineer ended with the outbreak of war, and after being a cavalry cadet, he transferred to aviation in 1915. His early career received a set back following an injury to his hand by a propeller blade, and when he did finally see action he crashed on 9 May 1916 after a fight, his observer being killed, and Gilsher losing his lower left leg. Despite this he transferred to fighters, and flying with the 7th Detachment on Nieuport 21s, claimed five victories between April and July 1917 – by which time he had also taken command of the unit. In gaining his fifth victory on 20 July in a fight with 15 German aircraft, Gilsher's aircraft was seen to break up and he fell to his death. He had been awarded the Order of St George 4th Class, The Golden Sword of St George and the Order of St Vladimir 4th Class.

Ens Nikolai Kirillovich Kokorin, in contrast, came from a working class family, born in Khlebnikovo in May 1889. He joined the army in 1910, and a year later requested a transfer to aviation, but it was not until 1914 that his wish was granted. At first he flew two-seaters, and for his work he was awarded the Cross of St George 1st Class, in April 1916, and in August was sent to the 4th Detachment, flying defensive sorties under Kozakov during the defence of Tarnopol. Kokorin scored four victories on Nieuports and one (his second success) with a Morane H. He was killed in action on 28 May 1917.

Ivan Orlov scored four Nieuport victories on the Russian Front with the 7th Fighter Detachment and one in a SPAD over France flying with *Escadrille* N3. He was killed in action on 4 July 1917

Capt Yevgraph Nikolaevich Kruten came from Kiev, having been born into a military family in December 1890. In 1901 he attended the Kiev Military Cadet Corps School, and was sent to a mounted artillery in 1908 and commissioned in 1911. He became an air observer in 1913 but soon trained as a pilot, and when war came he flew reconnaissance and bombing sorties, winning the Order of St Anne 4th Class in 1915 after downing a hostile aeroplane flying a Voisin. Kruten's unit, the 2nd Detachment, received Nieuports in 1916, and flying a Type 11, he scored two victories that August. He was then attached to N3 *Escadrille* in France, where he is said to have scored a SPAD victory in February 1917 and on returning to Russia, claimed three more victories with a Nieuport 17 as commander of his 2nd Air Combat Group. On 19 June 1917, returning from a war patrol, Kruten crashed near the airfield and died soon afterwards. His other awards were the Order of St Vladimir 4th Class, with Swords and Bow, the Order of St George 3rd Class and the French *Croix de Guerre*.

Another pilot with the 19th Detachment was Ernst Krislanovich Leman, a Lithuanian, born in 1894. He learnt to fly in 1916. With the 19th in 1917 he scored five victories flying a Nieuport, four being shared. Leman was awarded the Cross of St George 4th Class, the Order of St Anne 4th Class, then the Order of St George 4th Class and the Order of St Stanislav 3rd Class with Swords and Bow. Wounded in action on 26 September, he returned to the front just prior to the Revolution, following which he committed suicide on 17 December.

Lt Ivan Aleksandrovich Loiko, from Minsk, was born in February 1892 and joined the military in 1909. Following service with the infantry he transferred to aviation, flying reconnaissance sorties with the 30th Corps Detachment, which he later commanded in 1916. However, Loiko then went to the 9th Fighter Detachment, and with a Nieuport 11 had scored two victories by the end of the year. In 1917 he was flying a Type 17, adding three more kills and three probables to his tally, and his sixth and final victory was in a Nieuport 23. He received several decorations, including the Order of St Vladimir, the Order of St Anne, the Order of St Stanislav and the Rumanian Order of the Star, but his fate after the Revolution remains obscure.

Lt Donat Aduiovich Makeenok came from the Polish-Russian border country, born in May 1890. Enlisting in the Russian army in 1911, he transferred from the infantry to aviation and became a pilot pre-war. After flying two-seaters, he requested a transfer to fighters and saw duty with the 7th Fighter Detachment in 1917. Flying Nieuport 21s and 23s, Makeenok gained eight victories, his fifth on 29 June – he was the only Polish-born ace of World War 1 to fly against the Central Powers. He saw service during the Russo-Polish war in 1921, but information on his life after this time is not known. Makeenok had received the Cross of St George, the Order of St Vladimir, the Order of St Anne 3rd and 4th Class and the Order of St Stanislav 2nd Class with Swords.

Ivan Aleksandrovich Orlov, from St Petersburg, was born in 1895. He built gliders in his youth, and then a powered monoplane in 1913. By June 1914 he held a Russian flying licence, and after the war began flew Voisins. Becoming a fighter pilot in early 1916, Orlov flew with the 7th Fighter Detachment, gaining three victories with the Nieuport 11 by the

This Nieuport 11 (N1324) of *Escadrille* N35 was shot down by Kurt Student on 6 July 1916. Quickly repaired, the fighter was later flown by the German pilot in combat. Note that a Spandau machine-gun, larger windscreen and an anemometer ASI (on the left 'V'-strut) have been fitted by the Germans (*via Greg VanWyngarden*)

end of the year. Attached to N3 in France, he gained one SPAD victory in January 1917 and returned to the 7th, where he became an ace in a Nieuport 17 on 21 May. Orlov died in combat on 4 July during a fight with four German aircraft, the lower starboard wing of his Nieuport coming off. He had received the Order of St George, the Golden Sword of St George, the Order of St Vladimir, Order of St Anne, Order of St Stanislav and the French *Croix de Guerre*.

Ens Aleksandr Mikhailovich Pishanov came from the Crimea, born in October 1893. He took an interest in aviation whilst at engineering school and became a pilot in 1913. He fought with the army once the war started, but soon joined the aviation service. Posted to the 10th Fighter Detachment, flying Nieuport 11s Pishanov downed his first enemy aircraft on 21 March 1917, and by 7 July had scored five kills. Wounded

Lt Gustav Leffers of *Jasta* 1 flew this captured Nieuport 11, fitted with a synchronised Spandau gun. There is a suggestion that he was shot down in this machine on 27 December 1916 by a No 11 Sqn FE 2b (*via Greg VanWyngarden*)

Yet another captured Nieuport, this time a Type 23 from No 60 Sqn, which was brought down on 6 May 1917. Future ace Uffz Paul Bäumer flew several 'front flights' in this machine, adorned with a '7' on the fuselage and under both wings. This marking was added almost certainly because Bäumer was then flying with FA 7, prior to joining *Jasta* 2 in June 1917 (*via Greg VanWyngarden*)

four days later, he lost fingers from his right hand which ended his fighting career, although he later served with the White Russian forces and the RAF. In 1926 Pishanov emigrated to the USA, working for the Sikorski company as an engineer, and later with Seversky. He became an American citizen and died in 1966.

Born in October 1894, Capt Konstantin Konstantinovich Vakulovsky was yet another nobleman engineer. In the army pre-war, he transferred to aviation and was at the front in 1915. As the war progressed he served with the 33rd Corps Detachment and was then given command of the 1st Fighter Detachment in 1916. His first victory came on 7 September in a Nieuport 11. In all Vakulovsky scored six kills, five on Nieuports and one in a Morane-Saulnier I, his last two on 1 September 1917. Like so many others, little is known of him after the Revolution. He too won many awards including the Order of St Vladimir, Order of St George, the Golden Sword of St George, Order of St Anne and two Orders of St Stanislav.

The second highest scoring Russian ace (and on Nieuport Scouts) was Vasili Ivanovich Yanchenko, an ensign with the 7th and 32nd Fighter Detachments. Born on New Year's Day 1894, he was another engineer turned pilot. He moved onto fighters via two-seater recce aircraft, and with the 7th claimed his first success on 25 June 1916 in a Nieuport 11. His fifth and sixth victories were scored whilst flying a Morane-S on 13 April, but following a switch back on Nieuports, Yanchenko raised his tally to 16 by mid-October, by which time he was with the 32nd, which he joined in September. He fought with the White Russians in 1919-20, but after this went to America, where he worked as an engineer and became a US citizen.

APPENDICES

RFC and RNAS Nieuport Scout Squadrons in France in 1916-18

No 1 Sqn, March 1916 – March 1918
No 11 Sqn, March 1916 – July 1916
No 29 Sqn, March 1917 – April 1918
No 40 Sqn, March 1917 – October 1917
No 60 Sqn, August 1916 – July 1917
No 6(N) Sqn, December 1916 – June 1917

French Air Force Nieuport Scout *Escadrille* in 1915-17

N3, N12, N15, N23, N26, N31, N37, N38, N48, N49, N57, N62, N65, N67, N68, N69, N73, N75, N76, N77, N78, N79, N80, N81, N82, N83, N84, N85, N86, N87, N88, N89, N90, N91, N92, N93, N94, N95, N96, N97, N98, N99, N100, N102, N103, N112, N124, N150, N151, N152, N153, N154, N155, N156, N157, N158, N159, N160, N161, N162, N313, N314, N315, N392, N531, N561, N581

United States Air Service Nieuport 28 Squadrons in France in 1918

27th Aero, June – August 1918
94th Aero, March – July 1918
95th Aero, March 1918
95th Aero, May – July 1918
147th Aero, June – July 1918

Belgian Air Force Nieuport Scout *Escadrilles* in 1916-18

1 ére Escadrille, February 1916 – summer 1917
5 me Escadrille, September 1916 – autumn 1917

Italian *Squadriglias* in 1916-18

70ª, 71ª, 72ª, 73ª, 74ª, 75ª, 76ª, 77ª, 78ª, 79ª, 80ª, 81ª, 82ª, 83ª, 84ª, 85ª, 91ª

Russian Nieuport Scout Squadrons in 1916-17

1st, 4th, 7th, 9th, 10th, 19th, 32nd (Detachments)

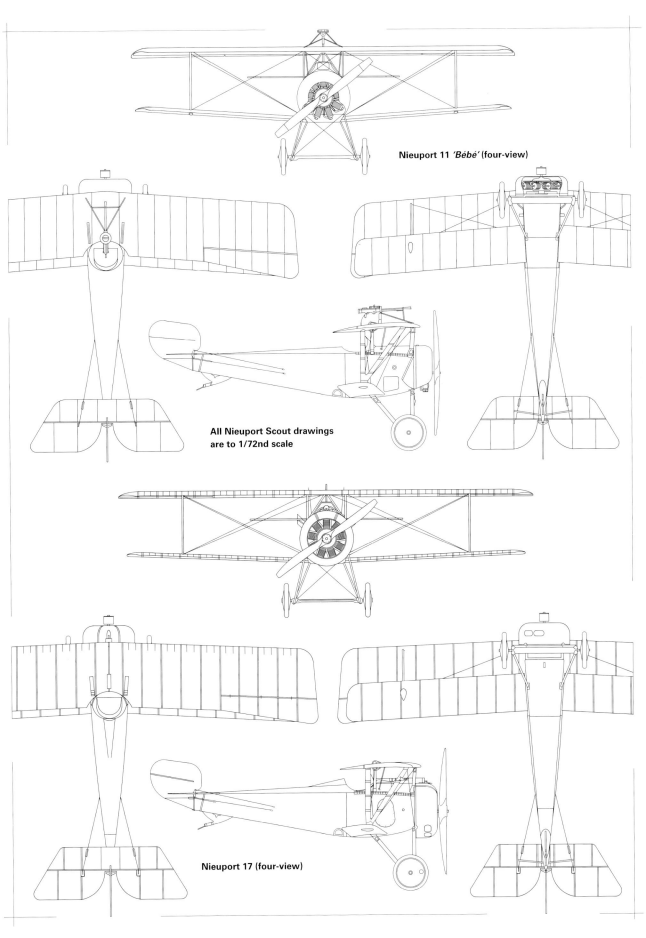

Nieuport 11 *'Bébé'* (four-view)

All Nieuport Scout drawings
are to 1/72nd scale

Nieuport 17 (four-view)

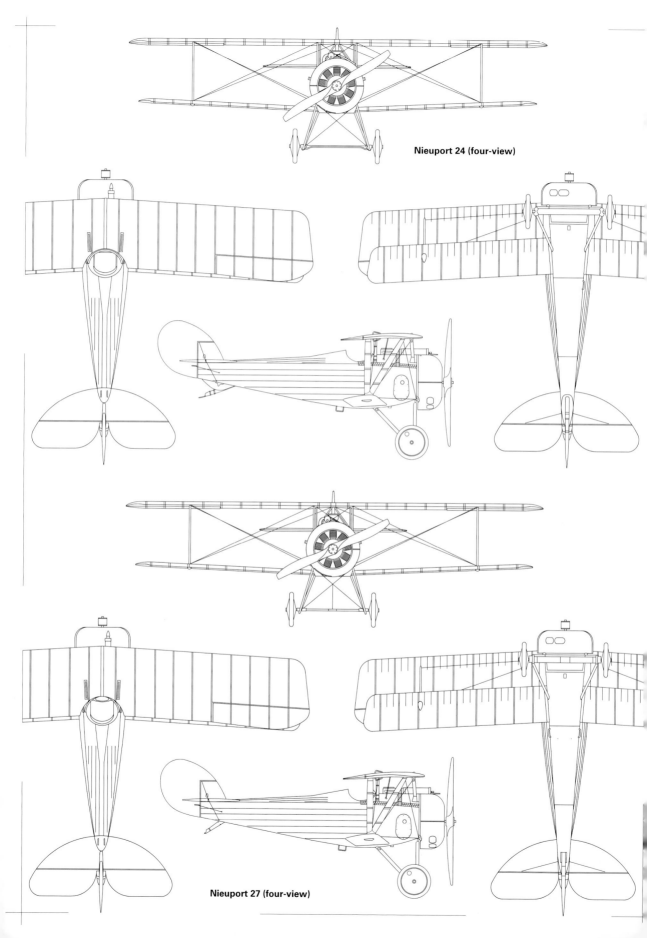

Nieuport 24 (four-view)

Nieuport 27 (four-view)

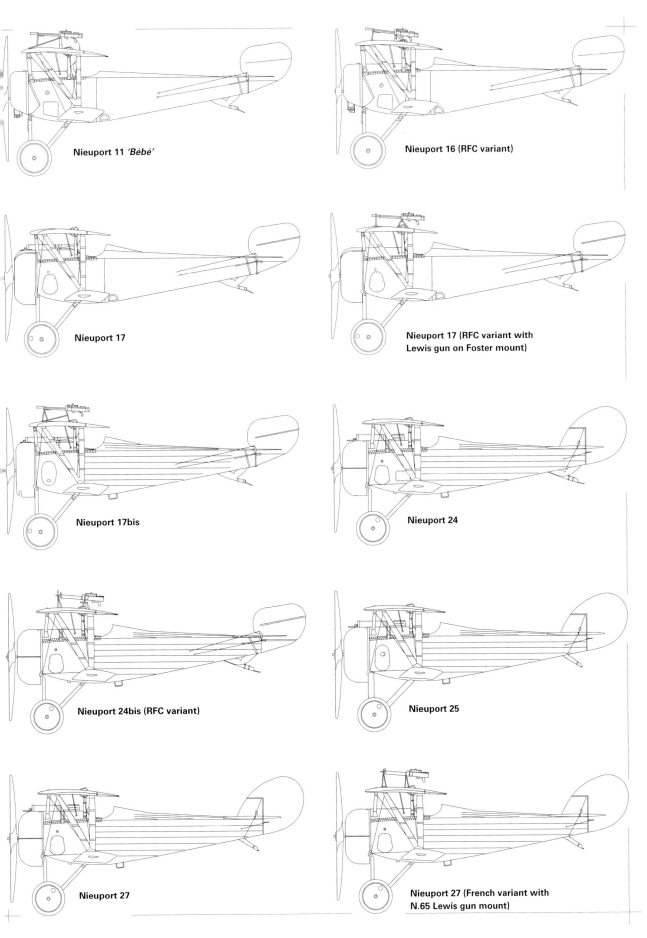

Nieuport 11 'Bébé'

Nieuport 16 (RFC variant)

Nieuport 17

Nieuport 17 (RFC variant with
Lewis gun on Foster mount)

Nieuport 17bis

Nieuport 24

Nieuport 24bis (RFC variant)

Nieuport 25

Nieuport 27

Nieuport 27 (French variant with
N.65 Lewis gun mount)

COLOUR PLATES

1

Nieuport 17 B3459 flown by Capt P F Fullard, No 1 Sqn, summer 1917

Like the majority of French-built Nieuport Scouts, this aircraft came to the RFC in factory-finish silver (aluminium) dope, with any additional colours or markings being made at squadron level. Generally, the wing V-struts were left natural varnished wood, although the cabane and wheel struts were silver. By the time Fullard took over B3459 (French N2706), he had already achieved 11 victories, and he went on to score his next 16 in this machine between 17 July and 22 August 1917. He used it from new, the scout having been flown in on 14 July. 2Lt G B Moore crashed B3459 on landing on 11 September, and it went to No 1 Aeroplane Supply Depot (ASD), where it was rebuilt and later shipped to Egypt in February 1918. It was finally written off in a crash at No 5 Fighting School (FS) in Heliopolis on 15 September 1918. No 1 Sqn's usual distinguishing marking was a red stripe immediately aft of the fuselage cockade (or roundel), while individual marking was by number – in this case Fullard carried a large black '2' on the fuselage. His flight members at this period had red horizontal stripes painted on the engine cowling, although there are no known pictures of Fullard's aircraft to denote whether it too had these. He himself said he did not have them, which may have been another identifying mark – no red stripes denoted the flight leader.

2

Nieuport 17 B3474 flown by Capt W C Campbell, No 1 Sqn, summer 1917

William Campbell gained his final six kills on this machine (out of his 23 in total) during the latter half of July 1917. He was also wounded in this Type 17 (French N2780) on 31 July. Tom Hazell had flown it in from No 1 ASD on 16 July. In this machine, too, Campbell scored his second, third, fourth and fifth balloon kills, making him the first RFC balloon ace. Capt L F Jenkin MC later downed his 21st victory in it on 4 September, but it was badly damaged in a crash on 6 November. Repaired, B3474 also went to Egypt, and was finally struck off charge on 21 March 1919.

3

Nieuport 27 B3629 flown by Capt W W Rogers and Capt G B Moore, No 1 Sqn, autumn 1917

This aircraft features in the famous winter line up photo of No 1 Sqn's machines taken on 28 December 1917, although all the aircraft serial numbers have been censored in this view. However, a similar shot taken from the front has not been tampered with, and it clearly shows that this Type 27 was indeed B3629 (French N5402), with 'H' on the fuselage (repeated on the top fuselage decking), together with the red No 1 Sqn stripe aft of the roundel. This machine arrived at No 1 Sqn on 7 September, and 2Lt P Wilson gained his first victory in it on the 23rd. Wendell Rogers claimed two of his nine kills with B3629 in October 1917, whilst Guy Moore scored his sixth 11 days prior to the photograph date. He claimed another on 4 January 1918, which was his final kill on Nieuports. Moore then flew the machine to No 1 Issue Section on 24 January, and the following month it was re-

issued to No 29 Sqn, where it remained until 19 April. Three days later it went from No 1 ASD to England.

4

Nieuport 17 B1506 flown by Lt A W B Miller, No 29 Sqn, summer 1917

This machine (French N2956) was delivered to No 29 Sqn on 7 April 1917 and became the mount of Archie Miller. He was in C Flight, whose machines were denoted by a large 'C' and an individual number on the fuselage side beneath the cockpit, ahead of the fuselage roundel. Miller's number was '6', thus B1506, in which he scored all six of his victories, was marked '6C'. Miller was shot down and killed in this aeroplane on 13 July by Hans Adam of *Jasta* 6. No 29 Sqn's identifying mark was a broad red band around the rear fuselage. Flight Leader, Capt A S Shepherd, flew B1504, marked '1C', and he scored nine of his ten kills in that machine. In the photo of No 29 Sqn's line-up, A6787, marked '3C', had been Shepherd's machine on the occasion of his first victory, on 11 May 1917.

5

Nieuport 17 B1552 flown by Lt E Mannock, No 40 Sqn, early summer 1917

'Mick' Mannock scored his second victory in this machine on 7 June 1917, a month after gaining his first – more than four weeks would pass before he scored his third. B1552 (French N3540) had been flown in from No 1 ASD by Mannock on 20 April. In June it was flown by Lt G B Crole, and on 2 July he gained three victories in B1552 out of his final total of five. Capt A W Keen MC flew a similar machine to this (A6771), marked with a red '1', from June 1917 until it was brought down whilst being flown by another pilot on 12 August. In November B1552 was sent to Egypt and was finally scrapped at No 60 Training Depot Station (TDS) on 3 January 1919.

6

Nieuport 23 B3607 flown by Capt E Mannock, No 40 Sqn, late summer 1917

By the summer of 1917 Mannock had got into his stride after a slow beginning, and by the time he began to fly B3607, his score had risen to nine. Lt W MacLanachan had flown this machine (French N4697) in from No 2 ASD on 21 August, and Mannock's first of five claims in it came on 4 September, and of his six kills claimed that month, only one was scored in another machine. The Nieuport had a large pointed spinner on the propeller, reported to have eventually been painted yellow (perhaps mustard yellow). It is believed that this colour was chosen by Mannock to serve as a reminder to other squadron pilots of his slow beginnings – not helped by his defective eye – that may have been interpreted as him having 'cold feet'. His other identifying insignia was the two black streamers attached to the interplane struts. This scout returned to 2 ASD on 14 October, and in November went to No 1 Sqn. B3607 was lost on 9 January 1918 whilst being flown by Lt E W Skelton, who is thought to have collided with another Nieuport over enemy lines.

7

Nieuport 17 A213 flown by Capt A Ball, No 60 Sqn, summer 1916

Built as French serial number N1579, this aircraft was

received by the RFC on 3 August 1916. It was in turn delivered to No 60 Sqn on 16 September 1916 and taken over by Albert Ball upon his return from leave in mid-September. By this time he had scored 19 victories and received the DSO and MC. Ball had added a further 11 kills in this aeroplane by the end of that month, and with his overall score standing at 31, returned to England for a rest. A213 was lost in combat on 6 March 1917 whilst being flown by the CO, Maj E P Graves, who was shot down into the British lines by OffStv Wilhelm Cymera of *Jasta* 1 at 1350 hrs German time, south of Wailly. Nieuports purchased from the French before November 1916 were generally painted in French olive drab – a sort of greyish green – on upper surfaces and wheel covers, with aluminium or grey engine cowlings. Undersides were clear-coped. A213 carried a red *cône de penetration* (as seen in the photo of Ball on his return from France) and the fuselage lettering 'A' and 'I', split either side of the roundel. This was repeated on the top decking.

8

Nieuport 10 N328 flown by Lt Georges Guynemer, *Escadrille* N3, June 1916

This specially built Nieuport 10 was powered by a 110 hp Le Rhône engine. Clear-doped overall, with dark blue tapes on the fuselage, the scout's engine cowling and struts remained in unpainted metal, with wooden V-struts and tail skid. It did not carry French cockades on the upper wing surfaces and also had a unique headrest. *VIEUX CHARLES III* was applied in large letters on the fuselage, with the *III* applied beneath the two words rather than after *CHARLES* as shown on some drawings. This lettering was probably applied in blue. Guynemer flew N328 from Cachy prior to the formation of GC12.

9

Nieuport 17 N1531 flown by Lt Georges Guynemer, *Escadrille* N3, July 1916

By mid-1916 N3 was using its soon to be familiar *cigogne* emblem on its aeroplanes. None were more famous, or well known, than Guynemer's several Nieuport Scouts, each carrying a red stork on the fuselage, but with some slight variation. On N1531 the stork was red, with blue or dark grey feathers on wing and tail and black legs. The machine had an overall silver-doped finish, and his individual identification marking was a large red '2', repeated on the starboard upper wing. The *cône de penetration* was painted red, white and blue, and this machine had a one-piece cowling and large wrap-around windscreen. Painted on the top of the fuselage decking was a black pennant, starting just aft of the cockpit's elongated headrest. Note that this machine lacks Guynemer's usual *VIEUX CHARLES* by the cockpit, the pilot instead having these words written on black and white cloth streamers which were attached to the interplane V-struts. The centre section of the top wing had transparent Cellon panels to improve upward vision. The following month Guynemer also had N1530 adorned in similar finish, except that the top wing surfaces were camouflaged dark brown and a greyish-green, and the number '2' was in white, although it remained red on the silver fuselage sides. And although N1530 had a two-piece cowling, it again boasted a red, white and blue *cône de penetration* and black pennant painted on the top of the fuselage. Finally, on the starboard side of the fuselage the red

stork was applied slightly more forward than that on the port side.

10

Nieuport 17 N1532 flown by Lt Albert Deullin *Escadrille* N3, summer 1916

For a period the Nieuports of N3 were very similar in finish, and the only obvious difference was a pilot's individual aircraft number. N1532 was silver-doped overall, but carried an entirely red stork and a red '3' on the fuselage sides, the latter repeated on the top upper starboard wing. It too wore a black pennant painted on the top fuselage decking. In a photograph of this machine can be seen what appears to be a patch just aft of the number, above the tail skid.

11

Nieuport 16 (serial unknown) flown by Adjudant André Chainat, *Escadrille* N3, 1916

This machine was camouflaged in dark brown and greyish-green on all upper surfaces and fuselage sides, with clear doping underneath, and dark brown wheel covers. The cowling was left unpainted metal and the '6' was applied in white. The stork emblem was also white, with a red beak and legs, and was positioned slightly forward, just aft of the cockpit. Chainat had the motif *"L'Oiseau bleu 3"* ('The Blue Bird') painted in white lettering just above the stork on both sides of the machine. It would seem that this was Chainat's third machine, and by the time he was flying a SPAD VII he had the number '6' after the name!

12

Nieuport 17 (serial unknown) flown by Lt Joseph Henri Guiguet, *Escadrille* N3, 1916-17

Guiguet's aircraft all bore the name *"Petit Jo"*, and this was number two in the sequence. Silver-doped overall with a red stork and red '8', the latter was repeated on the top starboard wing. The motif *"Petit Jo II"* is in black beneath the cockpit. At this same period, Tenant de la Tour flew a similar machine, his number being '10' (also repeated on the top starboard wing), and with a red stork.

13

Nieuport 17 N1428 flown by Adjudant René Dorme, *Escadrille* N3, summer 1916

N1428 had an early one-piece cowling, and this, together with fuselage and upper wing surfaces, was painted in dark brown and greyish-green camouflage, with clear doped undersurfaces. Dorme flew white '12', and this appeared on the fuselage sides along with N 3's stork emblem and the words *"Pére Dorme II"*. N1428 also had a large, unusual, windscreen. The scout's wheel covers were painted dark brown. Finally, the 'N' prefixing the aircraft's serial number was omitted from the rudder.

14

Nieuport 17 N1720 flown by Adjudant René Dorme, *Escadrille* N3, autumn 1916

Dorme's *"Pére Dorme 3"* (note the use of a Latin 3 rather than a Roman III) was silver-doped overall, with a plain metal *cône de penetration*. As far as is known the individual number '12' was applied in red and repeated on the top wing, whilst the pilot also had a French Cross of Lorraine, in dark green, painted on the top fuselage decking. The stork insignia too is in red, with blue feathers on wings and tail. Dorme's name insignia was painted beneath the cockpit on both sides. Note too that this machine was equipped with a Vickers machine gun rather than a wing-mounted drum-fed gun.

15

Nieuport 11 N642 flown by Lt Pierre Dufaur de Gavardie, *Escadrille* N12, 1916

This scout was covered in clear-doped fabric, with an unpainted metal engine cowling. De Gavardie's personal marking was three broad red, white and blue arrowheads on each side of the fuselage. It had black tapes along the fuselage borders.

16

Nieuport 17 (serial unknown) flown by Sous-Lieutenant Henri Languedoc, *Escadrille* N12, 1916-17

The interesting personal markings on this machine unfortunately have not had their colours confirmed, but an intelligent guess depicts the camel as dark brown with light yellow attachments on a black base. The aircraft was silver-doped overall, and the '4' on the fuselage was presumed to be in red. Sadly, the reason for the names *LOU* and *CAMEL* are not known to this author.

17

Nieuport 16 N977 flown by Adjudant Maxime Lenoir, *Escadrille* N23, 1916

The fuselage and wings of this scout were camouflaged in dark brown and a greyish-green, with the wheel covers also being painted dark brown. Its undersides were clear-doped and the engine cowling was left unpainted metal. Personal markings comprised the word *MAX* in large letters, one each coloured light blue, white and red. Behind this was a broad white band around the fuselage.

18

Nieuport 17 (serial unknown) flown by Adjudant Maxime Lenoir, *Escadrille* N23, summer 1916

Lenoir's later Nieuport was silver-doped overall, with a plain metal engine cowling. A red stripe was painted lengthwise along the mid-fuselage sides beginning aft of the cockpit. This was also repeated on the top fuselage decking. Lenoir's personal marking consisted of a white oval, edged with red, containing his name and rank painted in black.

19

Nieuport 11 (serial unknown) flown by Lt Armand de Turenne, *Escadrille* N48, 1916-17

Similar to a number of early patriotic Nieuport fighter pilots, de Turenne had his Nieuport 11's fuselage painted entirely in the national colours of red, white and blue. In the white section he had his family coat of arms marked – a shield with diagonal red and golden-yellow stripes placed in the centre of a black hunting horn. Wings and wheel covers were clear-doped fabric, and the engine cowling remained unpainted aluminium. In a later Nieuport 17 (N2186), de Turenne had the family shield marked in a rear-facing (red?) pennant-shaped triangle, with the family motto on a scroll above it. N2186 was a silver-doped machine.

20

Nieuport 11 (serial unknown) flown by Lt Paul Tarascon, *Escadrille* N62, summer 1916

The actual finish of this machine was either clear-doped overall or pale blue-grey, similar to Guynemer's N836 (see profile 8). The cowling was unpainted and left in natural aluminium. Tarascon's personal emblem was a large rooster, possibly black with a red beak, comb and legs. Beneath the cockpit, in large letters, was the name *"ZIGOMAR"*.

21

Nieuport 24 N3588 flown by Lt Paul Tarascon, *Escadrille* N62, autumn 1916

By the late summer of 1916 Tarascon was flying *"ZIGOMAR"* 5. Again the Nieuport was in overall silver finish, although the personal insignia (the rooster, the name and the individual number '2' on the rear fuselage) was now probably applied in red. The scout was also fitted with a red *cône de penetration*. Tarascon's previous *"ZIGOMAR"* 4 (N1662) carried a black '2' aft of a single red fuselage band, the latter being situated midway between cockpit and tailplane. Again, the name and rooster was painted all red. The ace's rooster emblem was eventually adopted as the *escadrille* insignia of N62.

22

Nieuport 17 N1895 flown by Lt Charles Nungesser, *Escadrille* N65, early summer 1916

Nungesser flew a whole variety of Nieuports, some camouflaged and some, like N1895, silver-doped. Like most of the ace's other fighters, this aircraft bore his famous personal insignia of a black heart, edged in white, upon which was painted a white skull and crossbones, coffin and two candlesticks. Also, like some of his other machines, this fighter carried broad red, white and blue stripes on the upper wings (see cover painting), although other pilots had these too. Nungesser also repeated these stripes on the lower wings and across the top fuselage decking on several of his scouts. This is one of the earlier, if not the original, machine numbered N1895. He seemed to have an affinity with this number, perhaps even a strong superstition, for he also had this serial applied to several other Nieuports, including a 17(bis), a 24, a 24(bis) and a 25. Just how this was allowed remains unknown, or perhaps it shows how authority allowed its top aces to do anything.

23

Nieuport 11 N576 flown by Lt Jean Navarre, *Escadrille* N67, 1915-16

Another patriotically-coloured Nieuport was Navarre's machine, carrying broad red, white and blue bands around the fuselage from the rear of the cockpit to just forward of the rear elevators. The rest of the fuselage, and the wings, was covered in clear-doped fabric, which looked distinctly light yellow. The inspection panels just behind the engine cowling were painted pale yellow to match the doped fabric. The cowling was natural metal, while the wheel covers were red, white and blue circles - blue innermost. What fuselage tapes remained exposed were black, and the interplane V-struts and tail skid were varnished wood. Navarre also flew an 'all-red' Nieuport at the height of his fame, during the Verdun battles in 1916.

24

Nieuport 17 (serial unknown) flown by Adjudant Pierre Pendaries, *Escadrille* N69, 1916

This machine appears to have been painted with the early two-colour camouflage of dark brown and a dark greyish-green, randomly sprayed on. The undersides remained clear-doped fabric, but the wheel covers were greyish-green. The white star was Pendaries' personal marking, and was painted on both the fuselage sides and the top decking of the fuse-lage just aft of the cockpit. Top wings were also camouflaged, although the exact pattern is not known, whilst the interplane struts were dark brown. Undercarriage struts were natural metal and the V-struts and tail skid were varnished wood.

25

Nieuport 17 (serial unknown) flown by Lt Maurice Boyau, *Escadrille* N77, summer 1917

Boyau's elaborately decorated machine was silver-doped overall with an aluminium cowling. The actual colours of his personal 'snake' marking remain unknown, but it is assumed to be very dark green, with white eyebrows (or whiskers). The snake appears to be breathing fire, but it could also be swallowing an octopus! Whatever it is, this portion of the artwork appears to be brownish-red in colour. As far as is known there is no photographic evidence showing the tail of the snake, so the artwork seen in this profile is provisional.

26

Nieuport 27 N5690 flown by Sgt Marcel Gasser and Lt Marin, *Escadrille* N87, late 1917 to early 1918

This machine was finished in the standard French five-colour pattern of late 1917-spring 1918 camouflage that was also used on the American-flown Nieuport 28s, as well as the SPAD XIIIs. The five camouflage colours were chestnut brown, beige, mid-green, dark green and black, with ecru (light yellow) undersides. The *escadrille* marking took the form of a cat with an arched back. On camouflaged machines this was depicted in white, with red collar and whiskers, while on aluminium-doped aeroplanes the cat was black. Individual aircraft identification was done by number, with Gasser's scout being white '12', repeated on the top fuselage decking. William A Wellman, the future American film director who served with N87 (and who had three confirmed and at least three unconfirmed victories) flew a silver-doped Nieuport 17 with a black cat and the number '10' in red. He carried the name *Celia* (*Celias I* to *V*) beneath the cockpit of his fighter.

27

Nieuport 17 (serial unknown) flown by Lt Marc Ambrogi, *Escadrille* N90, late 1917 to early 1918

This machine carried both a Vickers and a Lewis gun. It was silver-doped overall and carried the *escadrille's* cockerel insignia, which had a partly black body and tail, with yellow with black flecks on its undersides, legs and wings, a red comb and crop and yellow beak. The scout's individual number was '4', probably applied in black (although this may have been blue in colour), while just aft of the cockpit Ambrogi had a 'heart of Jesus' pennant painted on the top fuselage decking – here depicted as a red rectangle. The interplane and wheel struts were silver in colour, and the V-struts and tail skid varnished wood.

28

Nieuport 17 (serial unknown) flown by Lt Gustave Daladier, *Escadrille* N93, 1917

This scout was silver-doped overall, with matching interplane struts, wheel struts and wheel covers. The unit's duck emblem was applied in white on dark camouflaged machines, but here it is seen in black. In either case, it also had a reddish-orange beak and legs. Individual identification was by numbers on the rear fuselage sides in red.

29

Nieuport 11 N1256 flown by Sgt Raoul Lufbery, *Escadrille* N124, 1916

Thought to be Lufbery's first Nieuport, N1256 bore the two-tone sprayed-on uppersurface camouflage seen on many early Nieuport 11s, 16s and 17s. This took the form of dark brown and a greyish-green in meandering large patterns on upper surfaces, while undersides were clear doped, or sometimes light blue. The cowling remained bright, unpainted aluminium, while the wheel covers were dark brown. Interplane struts were also brown and the V-struts varnished wood. Lufbery's personal insignia was a white *RL* monogram.

30

Nieuport 17 N1844 flown by Sgt Raoul Lufbery, *Escadrille* N124, October 1916

Soon after Lufbery had replaced N1645 with N1844, the unit's Indian head insignia (the so-called 'Seminole', although in reality no Seminole Indians used full-feathered head-dress) was adopted by N124. This first version differed slightly from machine to machine, depending on the whim of the artist. The later Sioux Indian head was more in keeping with the *escadrille's* fighting role, and had a more war-like expression. Lufbery's machine was silver-doped overall, had both Vickers and Lewis guns, and getting away from any reference to his name, carried three Indian 'coup' marks in red on the rear fuselage – not an 'E' as has sometimes been suggested.

31

Nieuport 28 N6164 flown by 1Lt Douglas Campbell, 94th Aero Squadron, spring 1918

This scout is painted in the standard French five-colour camouflage pattern. At this stage the US-flown Nieuports had the whole fin and rudder in red, white and blue, with the red being rearmost and the white covering all of the front portion of the fin. Individual aircraft were identified by white or dark numbers on the fuselage. Campbell also had a red and black petal design on the engine cowling, and he may have had this cowling pattern on N6158 (white '0') in which he scored most of his remaining victories. N6158 had previously been flown by Capt David Peterson, who claimed two victories with it.

32

Nieuport 28 N6169 flown by 1Lt Edward Rickenbacker, 94th Aero Squadron, 1918

All US-flown Nieuport 28s were painted in the French five-colour camouflage. At various times Rickenbacker also used aircraft '12' and '16', although this machine is marked '1' in white, shadow-edged in red. It had previously been used by Maj John Huffer, the 94th's first CO. The '1' was probably also repeated on the top port wing (white, edged red), and in black on the starboard lower wing underside. The fighter also had the red, white and blue fin/rudder colours, with red being the rearmost colour. This was now in keeping with the American wing cockades, which were red, blue and white as opposed to the French red, white and blue. Finally, 'Rick's' scout had a red, white and blue ringed cowling.

33

Nieuport 28 N6144 flown by 1Lt James Meissner, 94th Aero Squadron, 1918

To illustrate the number of changes that some aircraft went through, Jimmy Meissner's N6144, in which he scored his first four victories, was originally 'dark 14', but after 10 May this was overpainted and replaced with a white '8'. As '14', it also carried a Third Liberty Loan poster stuck to the lower right wing (20 x 30 inches), Rickenbacker's 'white 12' also being similarly adorned on both lower and upper starboard wings. In action, Meissner's machine twice shed its top wing fabric, on 2 May and 30 May. His red and silver 'lightning bolt' cowling also varied in application. After Meissner left to go to the 147th Aero, N6144 was flown by 1Lt R F Cates, who used it to share a victory on 1 July 1918.

34

Nieuport 11 (serial unknown) flown by Lt Jan Olieslagers, 1 ére Escadrille, 1916

Reputed to be the only camouflaged Nieuport in Belgian service, this aircraft was sprayed dark brown and a greyish green (very similar, if not the same, as some French machines) on all upper surfaces. It had 'light coloured' tapes – possibly clear varnished – along the wing and elevator edges, which gave a yellowish hue. The cowling remained unpainted aluminium. Belgian cockades were worn well forward on the fuselage, right beneath the cockpit.

35

Nieuport 23 N3625 flown by Lt Andre Demeulemeester, 1 ére Escadrille, 1917

This scout had all its upper surfaces painted in khaki drab, the fuselage sides, all undersurfaces and the wheel covers in silver dope, and the engine cowling in metal finish. the upper wing-roots of the lower wings were also silver doped. As the leader of Yellow Flight, Demeulemeester carried a yellow square on the top decking of the fuselage. A similar sized square was repeated on the fuselage sides just aft of the cockpit.

36

Nieuport 23 (serial unknown) flown by Lt Edmond Thieffry, 5 me Escadrille, 1917

Like Demeulemeester's machine, this aircraft had khaki drab on all upper surfaces and silver doped fuselage sides and undersides. The wing root area of the lower wings (covering at least two ribs) was silver doped too. The scout carried the red comet marking of the *escadrille* on the fuselage sides, and the wheel covers were white with a red stripe (on both sides of each wheel). A similar white circle with a red port-to-starboard stripe was painted on the top fuselage decking. The engine cowling remained in natural metal finish. Interplane and undercarriage struts were silver and wing V-struts and tail skid varnished wood.

37

Nieuport 11 Ni1431 flown by Tenente Francesco Baracca, 1ª Squadriglia, spring 1916

This aircraft was finished in clear-dope overall, which gave the machine a light beige fabric, including wheel covers. The inspection panels just aft of the cowling on each side were painted in light yellow to blend in with the fabric, but showed up slightly darker. Fuselage edging tape was dark in colour, possibly black. The engine cowling was left in unpainted metal, while the cabane struts were grey, as were the undercarriage struts. V-struts and tail skid were in varnished wood. The aircraft did not carry Italian cockades, but had a large underwing area of both port wings painted red, while a similar area under the starboard wings was green. Both centre areas were clear-doped. The machine carried a Lewis gun with an extension to the gun butt.

38

Nieuport 17 N2614 flown by Capitano Francesco Baracca, 91ª Squadriglia, summer 1917

This French-built Nieuport 17 was silver-doped overall (and with a silver cowling), with the Italian tricolour on its rudder and on the undersides of the wings. Again, it had no cockades on its upper wings. Baracca's personal emblem was a black prancing horse (*Cavallino Rampante*).

39

Nieuport 17 (serial unknown) flown by Sergente Cosimo Rizzotto, 77ª Squadriglia, 1917

Rizzotto's scout was silver-doped overall, including wheel covers, struts and cowling, whilst the wing V-struts and tail skid were in varnished wood. Without cockades, the fighter nevertheless wore the Italian national colours on its wing undersides – red to port and green to starboard. The *Squadriglia* marking was a red heart painted on the fuselage. Like Baracca's N2614, this machine was French-built.

40

Nieuport 17 (serial unknown) flown by Tenente Fulco Ruffo di Calabria, 91ª Squadriglia, spring 1917

This aircraft features the same overall silver-doped fabric as the previously-mentioned French-built Italian machines, and also has the same red and green undersides to its wings. The pilot's personal marking was a black and white skull and crossbones motif, carried on both sides of the fuselage.

Back cover

Nieuport 17 (serial unknown) flown by Capt Alexander Kozakov, Commander of the 19th Corps Detachment, early 1917

French-built Russian Nieuports wore a variety of fabric colours from clear varnish to chocolate brown, brown and green to beige, as well as silver dope. Russian cockades could be on the tail and/or fuselage, except where a pilot's marking either covered the whole tail, such as Kozakov's skull and crossbones, or was on the fuselage sides as with Yevgraph Kruten's helmeted head of a medieval knight. Kozakov's unit used a white skull and crossbones on a white rudder as its marking, whilst his machines all bore the opposite emblem of a black skull and crossbones on a white rudder to allow him to be recognised in the air.